Bringing Heaven to Earth

A Journey Into Grace & Gratitude

Lee Ann Laraway

Bringing Heaven to Earth

ISBN: 978-1-935125-29-7

Book printed in the United States of America

To order additional copies of this book go to:
www.rp–author.com/Laraway

To read more about Lee Ann go to:
www.LeeAnnLaraway.com

Robertson Publishing
59 N. Santa Cruz Avenue, Suite B
Los Gatos, California 95030 USA
(888) 354-5957 · www.RobertsonPublishing.com

Twenty percent of the net proceeds from the sale of this book is donated to Canine Companions for Independence in gratitude for my three service dogs: Isaac, Zinkle, and Jeannie.

Table of Contents

Acknowledgements

I would like to acknowledge the tremendous love and support that my family has given me so freely over the years. You have been there, through it all, and are as much a part of this book as I am. Thank you for providing me an on-going foundation for life.

I would also like to acknowledge Patricia WhiteBuffalo and Kristi Piper, whose metaphysical work continues to keep my body up and running. You have enhanced my ability to blend the two worlds, the physical and the non-physical, for spiritual growth and miraculous health. Without your steady help, I would never have been able to write this book.

A huge thank you to Parthenia Hicks, my content editor, for your outstanding skills and suggestions, and to my cousin, Jo Ann Patton, for your time and expertise in editing all that grammar and punctuation! And to Alicia Robertson at Robertson Publishing, you are a gem. Working with you has been heaven on earth.

Finally, a special thank you goes to Colette Baron-Reid. It was your insight and guidance almost three years ago that gave me the direction for the manuscript, so it is because of you that I now have this book in hand. Your encouragement and friendship have been a wonderful blessing.

Preface

Life is about learning, and good teachers teach their students to be lifelong learners. Although this goal relates to academic learning, a pursuit of knowledge continuing over the span of one's lifetime, it is also applicable to an even greater purpose: the kind of learning that contributes to our own spiritual awakening.

My life has certainly been about learning. When I was young, I was taught about academic learning and I excelled at it. By age thirty, however, I began to realize that the major focus of my learning had been "outside" of me, and I was in desperate need of inner wisdom. I had been through my share of crises in thirty years, having lived with a severe physical disability from an undiagnosed case of polio.

One Friday evening, as I was leaving the emergency room with a food obstruction still lodged in my throat, threatening my airway and my breathing, I finally knew I had to start taking charge and working with life—and my body— from the inside out. This was to be my final nightmare of dealing with my body medically from an outside point of view, through well-meaning physicians who "looked, but could not see." What I did not know was that this traumatic experience would be a turning point in my ability to elicit health and happiness in my life, despite progressive physical weakening. If my disability had been the catalyst for learning spiritual truth in this lifetime, this experience was the extra fuel needed to wait no longer to awaken. There would be no time to waste if I were to avoid further suffering with what appeared to be no solutions in sight.

There is something about serious health issues that commands our attention in a new way and has the potential to awaken us to something greater than ourselves for healing. After this and many similar experiences, I felt an urgent need to learn about energy and the metaphysical world so that I could deal with my physical challenges without such nightmarish results. The medical experiences in the first half of my life were fragmented and often painfully disastrous. However, they had set the stage for a major learning curve on my part—to blend the physical world with the metaphysical world.

My physical disability has definitely awakened me. It has taught me how to direct my strong will in a healthier way through intuition and guidance, to question my limits and what I believe to be reality, to see the interconnectedness of all, and how the effects of my thoughts create my world every day. I have often told people, "Thank God I got that optimistic gene from my mother!" It has been one of the many gifts from the Divine that has been tested often in this lifetime. It has propelled me to look for good, even when there seemed to be none in sight. It is still training me to see with a spiritual sight that opens possibilities that were never present with physical sight alone. And with that has come a deep sense of joy and peace, and a calmness about life that becomes more solid each day even during the most difficult situations. My awareness of Divine Grace and the ability to access it has been sharpened, and my gratitude, grown immense.

In this book, I share my life story with you since it is through our individual experiences of life that we learn. The tone of my writing reflects the progression and depth of my inner development over time. In my earlier years, I was outwardly observational and matter of fact, so my descriptions of life at that time are from a more mental, superficial perspective. As my inner quest progressed, so did the depth of my spirit and I found I could write about life from a more emotional and spiritual perspective.

I have experienced great suffering and tremendous Grace. Although you may be drawn to the painful parts of my experience as you read, I caution you against staying overly focused upon them, or attempting to find logic in them. Just as I discovered for myself, some answers will never be found with the mind. My most painful experiences often seemed to release unwanted, heavy energy and *turn me in another direction*. It is the Good that is most life-giving, and that is what deserves our greatest attention.

I refer to the healing energy of the Infinite, Source, God, or the Divine as a greater power for Good, or Grace, that exists in the universe. For me it has been a higher, immensely wise level of energy. It has had a profoundly positive effect and impact on my entire life, especially in the area of my greatest need—dealing with all aspects of living daily with a severe, progressive physical disability. We all emanate from this spark of the Divine regardless of religious preference, and we are, by virtue of this origin, already connected to It. The purposeful intention to expand into It and bring It forth consistently through our will into the physical plane is what brings peace to the body, mind, and to the world.

The final chapter of my book contains some of the main concepts that have been key in developing my ability to consciously bring forth and exist upon this higher, healing energy. You will see throughout my book that Grace sometimes appeared through my purposeful intention to find It, that sometimes the old beliefs and ways of living had to collapse before something better could be created, and that many times Grace just appeared to gently move me along, often unnoticed at the time but profoundly effective. I have seen for myself and through myself that Divine Grace is present everywhere and in every situation, but it is our job to call it forward to bring Light out of darkness. I hope this book inspires you to discover Divine Grace in your own life and the ability to consciously choose to bring its goodness to you.

Living with a physical disability has deepened my awareness of and interaction with the Divine for creating all aspects of my life. This has been the perfect situation to stimulate a mental quest for understanding the positive, expansive nature of life and has helped me repeatedly find solutions and relief when there seemed to be none in sight. Esoteric contemplation of the metaphysical and physical worlds without action would have been intellectually stimulating but not life-altering. True learning, true knowing, has come from repeated, direct application in real-life situations where my will to persist rather than succumb to fear has been invaluable.

Chapter 1

My First Misdiagnosis

It was as if they looked at me through a fun house mirror.
No matter how hard they looked, their perception was distorted.

I am certain that polio was the last thought to enter my pediatrician's mind in 1959 when I was brought into the emergency room with an extremely high fever and seizures. I was taken to the hospital after my mother had suddenly sensed that something was wrong and came in to check on my twin brother, Bill, and me. She quickly realized that I had a high fever and was having a seizure. We had just been put to bed a little earlier and my parents had sat down to visit and play cards with some friends in the living room. I was barely seven months old.

Unfortunately, the waiting room at the hospital was extremely busy so my family waited patiently for over an hour for the doctor. During that hour my fever unknowingly raged on, as did a polio virus, burning up motor nerves throughout my body. When I was finally seen, my pediatrician examined me and decided that the extremely high fever had been due to an ear infection and that the fever had also caused the seizures. A well-meaning physician sent me home that night with my first misdiagnosis. The virus and the extent of the widespread damage had not been recognized. My aunt Josephine, a nurse, had come to the emergency room to join my father after my mother, who had stayed home to take care of my brother, called her for help. Aunt Jo was relieved that by the time I returned home the seizures had stopped, though she noticed that my legs fell outward as they lay me back in my crib. She discarded her intuitive feeling of concern, telling herself, "Maybe she is just tired."

1

Large epidemics of polio, a dreaded disease that killed or disabled many thousands in the United States alone, occurred immediately after World War II. A highly contagious virus, it did not discriminate among ages. Nearly half a million children and adults contracted polio in the United States before the Salk vaccine was announced and disseminated in a nationwide immunization program in 1955 (and later replaced by the Sabin live-virus vaccine) to combat and eradicate the virus. It was so successful that by 1964 only 121 new cases of polio were reported.

The polio virus fiercely attacked specific neurons in the brainstem and the anterior horn cells of the spinal cord, leaving various levels of damage in its wake. Extreme muscle weakness and non-movement resulted, and depending upon the severity, breathing and swallowing difficulties resulted as well. The virus was so aggressive that many died, and those that did not were deemed, "Polio Survivors." The hardiest of souls survived to go on for treatment and rehabilitation.

Polio patients were immediately quarantined during the acute phase of the illness until their medical condition stabilized, and intense rehabilitation programs followed to deal with the aftermath of pain and weakness. Rehabilitation focused on increasing muscle function through exhaustive exercise, heat packs, and water exercise to stimulate new nerve growth. Patients were worked unceasingly and were pushed to their maximum potential over many, many months. Their hard work and diligence often brought back significant amounts of strength and function. Eventually this chapter of their lives could be set aside as they picked themselves up again.

I became ill after receiving the Salk vaccine. Although the damage I had suffered was widespread, the severity of the motor damage to my body was not immediately obvious possibly because I was so young and not crawling yet. I was even given the Sabin live-virus immunization when it came out in 1962 as a precaution, not knowing that the physical difficulties I was having were actually a result of polio. Essentially, the motor nerves to my muscles had "fried" and died back while my sensory nerves became heightened and more sensitive. No muscle sets were spared from significant damage.

My brother and I were very different in personality, as many twins are. I was the more easy-going, placid baby. My brother, on the other hand, was full of nonstop energy and curiosity. So when he began walking, or as my mother said, running, my parents thought I was just slower to develop. Other indicators of unusual weakness were present, however, including mild problems on occasion with swallowing food. My feet began turning outward from weakness, so the doctors tried casting them for a correction. This proved useless, since immobilizing already weak muscles simply made them weaker. My developmental milestones in other areas, such as communicating and potty training, were right on target but strength and motor skills continued to lag. Soon there was a large gap between my brother's skills and mine. My family was obviously concerned. I was taken to multiple specialists in the valley, but to no avail. One doctor suggested I might have muscular dystrophy, but most said I was fine and not to worry. The final doctor told my parents that I wasn't walking because they must be favoring me over my brother and that I was spoiled, with no reason to walk. My father was so outraged that he scooped me up and walked out of the office. That was the last office visit for quite some time.

People are often amazed that I don't resent the fact that life could have been different if I had received the right help. It certainly seems to be a justified feeling, but I am grateful it has not been a dominant one for me. It would have held me back, keeping me locked in a weighted past, and suppressed my ability to do life well. I cannot say I specifically worked on releasing resentment. I assumed early on that the repeated misdiagnoses were one of those unexplainable parts of life, possibly because this appeared to be my family's response to the events. I was never interested in fantasizing about the life I could have had (the one I could have erroneously assumed would have played out perfectly, of course). I knew at some deeper level that this *was* the life I was supposed to have, possibly because its circumstances were too bizarre to be an accident. Fortunately, I never believed I had gotten someone else's life by mistake and I don't remember ever comparing my life to someone else's and resenting what they could do. These thoughts of mine and of my family were, I'm sure, highly imbued with the wisdom of Grace. I don't recall my family focusing heavily on the injustices or reliving them from a victim's perspective, so neither did I. My parents' memory of specific details and time frames about these years is vague. This period was a confusing, surreal time for them and I think they eventually found some acceptance in realizing it would never make sense.

My brother and I with my mother.

I did learn to crawl but never walked. My legs were weaker than my arms, but even my arm strength was so impaired that I was never able to transfer myself. In fact, I would never dress, bathe, or use the bathroom independently. Since there was no formal diagnosis, the standard rehabilitation given to polio patients to rebuild nerve endings and increase muscle strength was not offered. As a result, I had the opposite experience. Instead of gaining strength and function, I appeared to lose more strength over time as my body grew and the weakened muscles worked harder and harder to move a larger body. I was almost four years old before receiving occupational and physical therapy on a regular basis, diligently sought by my family and Aunt Jo, who worked for the County Health Department.

Since the doctors had not identified a specific problem or diagnosis, my parents were on their own in those early years to deal with their child who had significant physical limitations. There was no one to coordinate or suggest medical equipment or ways to make life easier, since supposedly there was "nothing wrong." I was either carried or pushed in a stroller that had been specially made to fit my growing body. After starting formal physical and occupational therapy, I finally received my first wheelchair. This was needed to attend kindergarten since a stroller would just not do!

I now had some freedom and could push myself slowly, but independently, and I was definitely interested in doing things myself. At last with wheels I could turn and face in any direction of my choosing, and push myself on flat, hard surfaces. I had the strength to push for short distances around the house, in the yard, and eventually in the classroom. With more movement came the ability to engage more in life, and probably also the ability to get into more trouble.

Around this time, and in hopes of a diagnosis, I was finally seen at Stanford Hospital. I remember being up on a stage in front of a sea of medical students, a real life model along with my brother for comparison, while they had us do various movements. Apparently, my disability baffled them as well. The final result was more of a description than a diagnosis: "A polio-type virus" and "Flaccid Quadruplegia due to Polyneuropathy."

None of my friends or family were physically disabled, so I joined into daily life with the concept of life first, disability second. In other words, my disability was obviously part of the show, but not the main show. I had to do things differently, but I was not going to be left behind. Years later I remember being surprised when looking at myself on a videotape at how truly disabled I was. Because my thoughts were never in that arena, I did not perceive myself as being so limited. I know now that not seeing such limits helped maximize my potential in all areas, as it left doors open for Grace to enter. My soul was whole, my mind was whole, but my body was not.

However, anything used in excess by the ego and not grounded deeply in spiritual wisdom goes awry. What had been a strongly good approach to life became a double-edged sword when not wielded wisely, and came back in unhealthy ways years later. My strong will and drive to experience life fully as if I were not disabled overrode my body's needs, and I eventually had to learn many tough lessons about listening to my body and finding balance. Photographs I'd seen over the years had not reflected my weakening state and increasing struggles with movement, or maybe I just didn't want to look. My mind and personality by the time I was thirty years old were running the show. I was having a busy, productive life that would have been commendable for an able-bodied person. However, the amount of energy and focus that was needed was tremendous and my body was getting dragged along to try to keep up. Eventually it would catch up with me, and bring me the need for deep, spiritual learning.

Chapter 2

*My Disability Was Part of the Show,
But Not the Main Show*

Do the best you can with what you have.

My grandmother, Augustine Arbios, came to live with us in 1962 to help take care of my brother and me. She had already been taking care of us during the day from the time we were six months old so that my mother could go back to work as an elementary school teacher. My father eventually started his own business as a Chevron dealer and worked long hours, too, so the extra help was essential and greatly appreciated. Someone was needed daily to take care of us and eventually take me to therapy, swim lessons, and to school and back. Carpooling with other families was not an option, since therapy obviously was not an extracurricular activity for most children. Besides, I could not just hop into someone's car and go!

My grandmother was a strong, positive influence in my life, my "other" mother. Since my mother and her sisters worked, Gramma helped to raise many of my cousins at our house during the day. Ours was definitely a matriarchal family, and our house was Grand Central Station as family members came and went daily. Gramma had a clear sense of right and wrong, was a problem-solver instead of a complainer, and did not tolerate bad behavior or bad attitudes. She was a rock, tending to the myriad of tasks that a day brings and providing emotional stability for all with purposeful confidence.

Gramma was an intelligent, hard working, no-nonsense kind of woman with a good heart and high integrity that made her a natural leader. She had grown up on a farm in the French Alps, had begun working as a maid in one of the bigger cities in France at the early age of thirteen to help with the family finances, and was eventually sponsored by her uncle to immigrate to the United States when she was seventeen years old. She married a sheep rancher, who was also of French decent, and supported him fully by running their home, raising four children, and feeding the countless people who went along with maintaining a large sheep business. When her husband died suddenly in his early 40s, Gramma added to her life's responsibilities by running the sheep business for the following nine years until her youngest daughter, my mother, was ready for college. This was no easy task, and doubly so because she was a woman entering what was traditionally viewed as a man's world. I am sure this was one of the most frightening and exhausting times of her life, but she was undaunted and used her faith and her determination to create a safe, stable life for herself and her children. She did not need any New Age courses to teach her how to deal with fear and how to connect to her Source before she was able to act. She met the challenges head on. And in the functional reality of life, and by the way she chose to work with it, her soul was strengthened and deepened. She certainly demonstrated a mindset through example that would highly influence the way I approached life in the years to come.

In an attempt to provide my body some sort of exercise, my parents signed me up for private swim lessons at the age of two. Jim was to be my swim instructor for the next seven years. I went religiously three times a week, practicing different strokes as best I could while slowly kicking my feet. I remember feeling free in the water, enjoying movement from the buoyancy that I never had known on land. As I got older I was able to do less, but still was free to roll from my back to my stomach to swim, and to slowly pull myself up to a vertical position. My family tells stories of my very early years of swimming, when I supposedly swam the length of the pool underwater in one breath. To this day, my breathing is decreased but has remained amazingly functional and stable. My experiences in the water may have set the stage for stronger, more stable breathing later in life, or it could be that I just have a lot to say! I continued to enjoy playing and swimming in our small backyard pool with my brother and cousins during summers until I was 11 years old, when the unfortunate results of a poor spinal fusion left me permanently too weak to be independent in the water or to swim again.

The early years of daily exercise taught me discipline. The swim lessons continued until the age of nine and I had physical and occupational therapy twice a week until I was twenty-one years old. I also had a daily home program to stretch out my muscles as well as time out of my chair every afternoon so I would not grow into the shape of the chair. Attempting to walk with rubber braces on parallel bars led to more rigid braces and a stand-up table in the early primary grades, as I got weaker. Working on maintaining my muscle strength was addressed very strongly by my family as a primary focus along with school. Work first—even if it hurt—and play later. Most importantly, I was to approach it all willingly even if I did not feel like it because it had to be done. End of the story. I was learning that even though I was presented in life with some difficult things, I had the ability to work with them rather than resist them.

I think I accepted my routine well because I saw the same approach modeled regularly in a very matter-of-fact way by my family. This powerful expectation established another helpful building block toward my approach to life. Their expectations for teaching me self-responsibility were not lessened because I had a disability. In fact, the opposite was true. Also, doing what was presented in life without making a dramatic story about it was deeply instilled in me as a life skill. It would eventually give me the ability to run my life well independently as an adult, and the willingness to give the effort needed for even the simplest of tasks as well as handle the multitude of details needed to get through a day.

I am sure that my family felt extreme grief over all of the physical difficulties and mishaps that occurred repeatedly in the first half of my life, but they did not stay focused on it and, therefore, I was not tainted by its force. As a result, the energy that would have gone towards emotions like anger, pity, envy, sorrow, etc., was freed up to be used toward problem solving. Though I would need to learn some balance in feeling the range of emotions later, it was a base at that time that served me well. This not only taught me structure, organization, and discipline but it also empowered me over time to take charge of my life and not play victim.

My grandmother always said, "Do the best you can with what you have." This implied high standards without comparing myself to others. I remember at a very young age that I was to do my part, whatever I was able to do, and to do it well even if it took longer than anyone else (and it always did physically). Learning early on to be persistent and follow through gave me successes that were earned, and there is no better way to build self-esteem than that. I have memories of being as young as four, and after being dressed, sitting on my bed putting on my own shoes and socks. Now I'm sure it would have been faster for my family to do it, but that was not the point. I was contributing to my own care and not only learning responsibility, but also learning to be in charge of my life.

Around the same age, I also remember my mother reading me the book, *The Little Engine That Could*, on several occasions. I do not remember any other books that she read to us, but this one stood out in my mind because of its message. In the story, there was a train engine that made deliveries over the mountain. One day it could not, and the little blue engine, which was not very strong, volunteered to do the job. No one believed he could do it, but he persisted slowly repeating to himself, "I think I can. I think I can," as he chugged up the mountain. Though the original book had been written in the 1940s, it was full of positive thought, intention setting, and affirmations for manifesting what he wanted. Needless to say, he did what the others thought was impossible and the little blue engine saved the day. When my mother finished the book, she would tell me that I was like the little blue engine, and even if it took longer than everyone else, I could do anything I wanted to if I made up my mind. A profound teaching from a simple book and an intuitive mother delivered at a perfect time for me. I could relate to that little blue engine, and the lesson it taught resonated as Truth for me. Like the engine, having a positive attitude and being persistent in working toward goals in my own way and at my own pace were to become one of my strengths for being successful and happy throughout life despite many, many challenges.

Parenting is a difficult task, significantly compounded when dealing with a child's serious health issues. I have sometimes seen compassionate, well-meaning parents, however, take over and do everything for their disabled child (regardless of the type or level of disability) or make excuses for them out of grief or guilt. However, from my own experience I feel very strongly that this unknowingly causes a greater disability than the original one, for the unspoken message to the child is, "I can't." Knowing how my thoughts have had a very direct effect on my body's functioning and health, this is an incredibly devastating message to present to growing minds. I believe children with any kind of disability need to be taught to the best of their ability to be *more* responsible for themselves and develop healthy emotions for problem-solving by virtue of their challenges in life. This *enables* them instead of disabling them, and gives them greater opportunities in life to be successful.

The fact that this story about the little engine still stands out so strongly in my mind suggests how significant it was in supporting my emotional development, and most obviously to me, how it was divinely guided. Sometimes we solicit guidance through meditation and prayer and take an active role in attending to its outcome. More often, however, I believe that support and guidance is given in life freely through Grace without our conscience solicitation. I also believe that the more we become aware of It and the more grateful we become, the greater the pathway becomes to receive more Grace. Many times we are unaware in the moment of how significant the support is, or that we even need it, until we look back over time and see its influence. Thank goodness I have experienced this over and over again in my own life and have become deeply grateful for its effortless wholeness that softens life and helps to balance the darker, more traumatic periods.

As a child, I did not know about asking directly for divine support and guidance. We attended an Episcopal church regularly throughout my elementary school years where meditation was not discussed and prayer seemed stilted and certainly not very personal for me to a God far away. I was spurred on as an adult by a history of physical traumas to step into the metaphysical realm and engage more consciously with the healing energy of the Universe. I learned to specifically and repeatedly elicit divine guidance and Grace to support my weakening body, to obtain more peaceful outcomes from medical procedures, and to get my needs met more easily in life. Basically, I eventually realized that I had to develop my inner world to more gently and safely create my outer world, rather than force my body to do life through teeth clenching and sheer strong will.

Chapter 3

Fitting In

Status. I had become good at leaning over and tossing those marbles from my chair as opposed to shooting from the ground.

Looking back, I am now aware of many pivotal events that were key in opening my life's path toward functioning well in a non-disabled world and that eventually led me into a vocation that serves others. These events, so perfectly sent, fell into place naturally and without effort. They were truly Grace given. Their ease was a relief from some of the not-so-easy aspects of life.

The first such event that stands out in my mind was the decision regarding where I was to go to school. I entered kindergarten before there were laws that support education in the least restrictive environment. In those days, children were sent to special schools if they were physically disabled regardless of their abilities. There was an orthopedically handicapped school connected to the site where I attended weekly therapy, and most likely I would have attended that school if it had not been for a simple statement made by the school's principal when my parents met with her to seek advice: "Why don't you try her in public school first if they will accept her, and if it does not work, she can always come here." I was fortunate that my local school district was progressive and willing to let me attend in a time when most districts shied away from this kind of inclusion.

The only adaptation I needed was a table to use as a desk that followed me from year to year through elementary school. My grandmother was the chauffeur, taking my brother and me to and from school each day, as well as bringing us home for lunch so that I could use the bathroom. These were the days before modified vans were available, so I had to be physically lifted in and out of the car and my wheelchair was folded and placed in the trunk. My grandmother was such a strong woman on many levels. Not only did she have the strength of character to do this and many other responsibilities every day as if it were something everyone did, but she was also physically strong and was still lifting me in and out of the car in sixth grade when she was seventy years old and I was a little over five feet tall and weighed one hundred pounds!

Having a physical disability as significant as mine affects everyone in the family and deepens them as well, I think. My brother, Bill, had to come home at lunch each day, too, and also spent many, many hours along with some of my cousins waiting for me each week in therapy instead of playing with his friends. He had extra responsibilities around the house to help make life work well. When he was old enough to drive, he took over driving me around so I could get to school and therapy until I was able to start driving myself years later in graduate school. I am sure that at the time he would have liked to have changed some of the things that made his life difficult, but he did what needed to be done, as did we all. Though the high demands of life were limiting to him in many ways, he grew up less egocentric as a result of them, and this remains a dominant characteristic of his personality today, especially when it comes to helping others. And as for my parents and my grandmother, they learned to take life as it came and to work through it to the best of their ability. These dynamics made for one strong family unit.

School was easy for me and I enjoyed it. I was the only child in a wheelchair in my elementary school, but I made friends easily and don't remember ever having trouble fitting in. Our school population was very stable so I basically went to school with the same group of kids from kindergarten through sixth grade. I do not recall any bad experiences getting teased by the other children for being different, possibly because *I* really didn't feel any different from them except for the fact that I did things sitting down. I was comfortable with who I was, and that acceptance may have rubbed off on them. I have met people since then with far less of a disability than I who were not as fortunate and who were teased enough to make them unsure of themselves even into adulthood. Having good friends has been a gift in life that I will always be grateful for. Social interaction was not to be a struggle for me, thank goodness. I never found myself spending too much energy in social drama even in high school, which gave me more energy to deal productively with life.

For the most part, I did what everyone else did in elementary school, especially in the classroom. The work was not too difficult and I still had enough strength in sixth grade to independently navigate myself around the room in my manual chair on those old, square tiled floors. Thank goodness for tile and not carpeting! I was never strong enough to push my chair on the playground, but I had a couple of good friends that could. Janet and Joan were identical twins and we paired up in friendship quite early on, from the beginning of first grade. As girls, we had no trouble walking around and just talking — or rolling around and talking! The boys were into physical sports and the girls were into chatting, which was right up my alley. I did other things with classmates, too. There was tetherball and two-square when I was younger, and playing marbles with mostly boys in the dirt yard by the classrooms in fourth grade. I had some pretty cool marbles including a few highly prized "steelies" which were actually truck bearings that my father had gotten for me from his gas station. Status. I had become good at leaning over and tossing those marbles from my chair as opposed to shooting from the ground. I got so good that one time one of the boys who lost told the teacher it wasn't fair because I wasn't shooting from the ground. The teacher said it was a reasonable adjustment and that it took skill to do it that way, so my marble career was allowed to continue.

There were other things I could not do, like participating in field trips and physical education. I probably was upset about these things, but my mother, the eternal optimist, constantly redirected me to focus on the good instead of allowing negative thought to ruin a situation. She was straightforward in explaining my options, and was always clear in teaching me that the responsibility for my happiness was mine. So if I could not go on the field trip, I was to find something good about spending the day in another classroom. If I could not play team sports with the class, I could watch the game and find enjoyment there. And so I did. She was right. There is pleasure if you know how to look.

One day in fifth grade as my friends and I were at recess walking and talking about who knows what, I was suddenly approached by a woman I had never seen before. She was dressed like she could have been a teacher, but I knew all the teachers and she was definitely not one of them. Seemingly out of the blue, she told me that she was a speech therapist, and that I should look into being a speech therapist someday, too. She said something about my having good speech and language skills. I remember nothing else about the conversation nor would there be any future discussions with her about the topic. In fact, I never saw her again. It always stuck in my head, however, and years later I did become a very successful school speech/language therapist. It was to be my vocation in life, a life's purpose that came creatively and effortlessly for over twenty years in the Oak Grove School District in San Jose, California.

So who really was that woman, anyway? Could she have been heavenly sent specifically for the purpose of giving me direction? It was an unusual conversation, or direction, from someone I did not know. The fact that I remembered this interaction when I was looking for a major in college speaks to its profundity. It was to be another obviously pivotal event that was sent to guide me in life.

I was physically healthy despite my disability. As kids we spent lots of time playing creatively outside when the weather was good. We often spent weekends and extended time during the summer at our cabin in Lake Tahoe. Many years later I would be able to enjoy the freedom of independent movement with my power wheelchair to "roll around in the dirt" and go off on my own, but during those early years I was much more limited in this way. Nevertheless, we had a wonderful community of friends and relatives whose families also had cabins nearby and who were more than willing to have me participate and push my chair.

Sitting in the middle of the sled at Tahoe with (clockwise) cousins Brian, Joni, Kathy, and my brother, Bill. This photo was taken the winter before my back surgery.

I loved the feel of the mountains, the smell of the trees, and the blackness of night. I especially enjoyed jeep rides into the more remote areas to look at the wild flowers, the streams, and occasional trips to a few of the small lakes. This was a way to give me a taste of being in the wilderness, and I am very grateful to my family for giving me these experiences. My parents could have been too scared to take me if they had focused on all of the things that could have gone wrong in those forested areas with someone as weak and immobile as I was. They met the challenge, however, by going on the longer trips with other friends in jeeps, letting people know where we were going, and taking my foldable chair. I had many, many enjoyable trips that could have been unrealized by fear, a fear that could have prevented the willingness to take calculated risks. I was, and still am, so attracted to the outdoors that there would be an empty space within me if these trips had never happened. Get my chair on that dirt and get me connected to a sense of the Infinite. To me there is no better way to connect with the Divine than in nature, and I know now that I felt that Presence way back then. The benefits for me far outweighed the risks.

Off for a jeep ride in the Stebbins' jeep. My chair fit exactly between the seats, giving me better stability for sitting.

Chapter 4

I Should Not Be in That Much Pain

I do believe now that the circumstances surrounding my onset of polio and my back surgery served to bring forth several major issues that my soul had come to earth to heal.

Although I worked hard at maintaining my physical strength, it continued to lessen a little each year as I grew. My muscles found it harder and harder to move a bigger body. Some muscles grew tight. The biggest challenge by the time I was eleven was my scoliosis, or curvature of the spine, that had occurred because my back muscles were too weak to support my bone growth. Several years of bracing my torso with a customized "corset" to keep me as straight as possible had helped but was not sufficient. The doctors were concerned that if the curve worsened, my breathing would be permanently compromised. The recommendation was a complete spinal fusion. I was healthy, my spine was flexible, and I was a good candidate for an excellent correction. The year was 1970, however, and spinal fusions were not as common or refined as they are today. Locally, Stanford Hospital was an option but they only performed a few of these surgeries a month. My parents were told of a Southern California hospital that had extensive experience with performing many such surgeries each week. The hospital, however, was almost six hours away and I would have to be hospitalized for six to nine months.

Since I was only eleven years old, I was not aware of how difficult a decision this was as my parents weighed the options. Having the surgery locally would allow daily visits from family, throughout the extended stay, but the expertise of the other hospital implied the best outcome physically. This surgery was to have a major impact on maintaining my respiratory functioning, so it needed to be done right. There is no question that this would strain everyone involved, and that I would have to be strong enough emotionally to live away from home and be strong enough physically to deal with the pain and recuperation of major orthopedic surgery with the support of weekend visits from my family. After a couple of appointments at the hospital and I am sure many, many sleepless nights on the part of my parents, I was scheduled to begin my stay there, missing the last two and a half months of my sixth grade year in school.

I was very naive about how I would feel being away from home and how traumatic this kind of surgery would be for me. My parents were obviously upset about having to leave me. Both dissolved into tears, including my father whom I don't think I had ever seen cry. I did not understand the depth of their despair. After all, how many kids got to leave school and live away from home for a while? I was looking forward to a little bit of independence and certainly did not want to see them sad. I remember consoling them as they left, reassuring them that I would be just fine. In fact, to me it seemed like a little adventure, a trip away from home!

Well, that self-assured stance lasted about an hour or so after they left. There are not too many events that I remember from my childhood with great detail, but I vividly remember feeling a sudden pit develop in my stomach, as if the bottom had dropped out, and an overwhelming sense of loneliness and despair that I'd never experienced before. It was such a foreign feeling that I had no words for it, so I completely shut down because I was not sure what was happening. I could not look or talk to anyone for several weeks for fear I would cry. I must have already learned by that age to hold back tears during painful experiences, and I was not going to let the other kids see me cry. I was the youngest on the ward by at least two years or more. Most of the patients were teenagers, and many were veteran residents, so I did not want to look like a baby. It took all of my will, but I held it all in and just nodded my head when I had to respond.

I did not know at the time that my parents had almost turned around to come get me, so upset about leaving me that they wondered if they had made the right decision. Two days later they showed up unexpectedly, flying in for a brief visit to console themselves, I think, as well as me. None of us could hold back our tears. Even though I was distraught, I knew, as did they, that this hospital stay had to happen and that we all had to be strong enough to do it. I'm not sure where that maturity came from on my part, but there was never a thought in my mind that I would not/could not do it.

Talk about a culture shock. Although I was obviously disabled, I had always been immersed in a non-disabled world at home, at school, and in the community. My only exposure to the world of disabilities had been seeing the other children receive therapy each week in the room with me. I did not feel an automatic connection or camaraderie with them just because of our disabilities. I was now surrounded at the hospital by teenagers and young adults ages thirteen to twenty one, with a variety of orthopedic handicaps, but I felt so different. Each room housed six patients and I was the only one in my room who had attended a regular education school. In fact, I may have been one of the only patients on the entire ward who had not attended special schools or lived some, if not all, of my life in a hospital. I was shocked that regular school had not even been a consideration for them, especially since several were only paraplegics and had significantly more upper body strength than I. We lived in the same state, yet our experiences were so different. The girls in my room all appeared to me to be of average intelligence, mind you, but their limited experiences had most certainly held them back academically, and probably socially. Two of the older teenagers in my room had lived at the hospital their entire lives. I was so grateful that I had not been held back just because I was weak, and felt badly for them that they had not been given the same chance. Needless to say, we had very little in common and I was determined to get back home as soon as possible.

My family visited every weekend during my entire stay. They had purchased a new Buick station wagon, a stylish 70s gold with wood grain sides, in preparation for the weekly treks. After working all week, they would leave very early Saturday morning and drive to arrive at the hospital by 10 a.m. Renting a motel room at the same little place each Saturday night not too far away, they came back to visit Sunday morning at 10:00 a.m., and left by 2 p.m. that afternoon for the long drive home. My grandmother and brother came each weekend with my parents until the last couple of months. They knew it had been hard for my brother to come and sit around every weekend, so they thought it would be better for him to stay home with my grandmother. As a child I did not truly appreciate the devotional and financial commitment and sacrifice made by my family. I was too busy trying to cope myself. Everyone did whatever they could to make the situation work, but you can only imagine the emotional and physical load for all of us. No one complained, but the stress was high and would continue for many years afterwards as we dealt with the permanent problems resulting from a surgery gone wrong.

My first month at the hospital was spent attending occupational and physical therapy and an in-hospital classroom, as well as a multitude of medical tests involving every part of my body. I was X-rayed, poked, prodded, and stuck with needles for blood draws and contrast studies. It is clear to me now that I was being studied for far more than my spinal fusion. At times it was scary because I never knew what test they would do and how much it would hurt. The previous years of therapy, bracing, and exercise routines had disciplined me to deal with unwanted tasks and pain so that I could move on to something more pleasant, but this was so different and I was by myself. Nevertheless, I did what I was told because that was what I had always been taught to do. Anything to make the surgery go well and recuperate quickly so I could go home sooner. The facility was relatively new, the nursing care was kind, and the therapeutic recreation department had regular activities and socials for the patients and their families. I wanted nothing to do with any of it. I just wanted out, and set my whole focus on doing whatever I could to shorten my stay. You know how committed I was to this goal when I tell you that I even ate liver when they served it because my mother told me I had to eat to get well, even if I did not like it!

For the entire first month, I had been free to leave the hospital on the weekends. It was a relief to be "semi-normal" again on those two days. My parents took us somewhere each weekend so my brother and I could have some kid entertainment. There was a wonderful ice cream and candy shop called "Helen Grace" in the shopping center next to the motel and every Saturday night we savored the most delicious ice cream sundaes with homemade ice cream served with a small warm jug of thick hot fudge or caramel topping, also homemade. They had the obligatory piles of whipping cream and a cherry on top, and we thought it was, as my aunt Yvonne would say, manna from heaven. I'm sure it was indeed heaven sent, as we needed something pleasurable to soothe us during this very hard time. It still brings back one of the only pleasant memories of that whole hospital experience. So much so, in fact, that my brother recently found a way to order their toppings online for us to enjoy once again.

But at the end of the first month, life was to change again. They brought me a different bed that looked more like a frame with a stretcher than a bed. This was where I was to be for the next four months. It was a striker frame, a special bed that allowed the staff to turn me over every few hours by strapping another "stretcher" piece on me so I was like a human sandwich, and then rotating the "sandwiched" me to my back or my stomach. An opening permitted me to look straight down at a little table below. I was then placed in traction that pulled from my head and my hips to straighten the curve in my spine as much as possible for over a month before surgery.

That ended our outings, and things continued to get harder and more painful for me. The traction gave me terrible back spasms, and there is not much to do or talk about when you don't get out of bed. I watched TV, listened to the radio, and played solitaire with a mini deck of cards when I was face down, waiting for time to pass. A teacher came to my bedside and we did some reading each day to finish out the school year, but I was completely unchallenged and definitely unmotivated. I was fading into an institutional life where the day is structured by physical needs rather than stimulating life experiences, and each day crept by slowly. I obviously was not a brilliant conversationalist either by the time the weekend rolled around and my family came to visit, and I began feeling detached from life at home.

I was so ready by the time the surgery date arrived. This was what I had come to do. I don't remember much about the few days leading up to surgery except that I wanted to have this part finally done so I could move on, heal, and get back home. I had no idea what to expect physically, but I was tired of waiting. I was ready for a change. I remember that morning being rolled outside across the grounds on a gurney from the new children's building where I had been living for the past two months to the old, main building with long, dreary hallways for the surgery. The prep seemed to take forever. After multiple failed attempts by a young nurse to place an I.V. in my hand, someone finally came over to take charge and placed the needle on the first hit. I remember thinking that the first nurse must have been in training and wishing that they had assigned me someone with more experience instead of having to become someone's pin cushion.

I woke up after surgery with heavy nausea and the most excruciating pain I had ever felt. Past experiences with the pain of broken bones and sprained muscles could not light a candle to this. And as if that were not enough, there was bad news as well. My mother told me that the doctors had not been able to finish the surgery and stopped after almost seven hours so I would not lose any more blood. In fact, they were only half way done. She told me their plan was to repeat the surgery in two weeks, take out the metal rod, and start again. It felt like another weight had just been added, but I was in so much pain that all I could do was deal with the moment. My parents were masterfully calm and reassuring for my sake, but I could tell they were distraught by the sadness in my mother's eyes and the way my father looked silently away, furious at the world. I dozed in and out of painful sleep for the next several days in intensive care, and recall during one of the visits how my mother just stood holding and patting my hand as she gazed off, lost in thought.

The second surgery did not have the best outcome, either. Much to their surprise, my spine had already fused to the metal rod and it could not be removed, so they had to scramble for a quick and unexpected "Plan B." Another half rod was added with a make-shift union between the two that unfortunately did not hold and ultimately released sometime after surgery before fusing, creating a worse curvature than when I started despite casting for the next three years. No one knew why, but it took several years for my back pain to dissipate.

No one could explain why I had lost approximately 70% of my strength throughout my entire body that was never to return, either. I had been given therapy. They had not seen that problem before, they said, and I should not be in that much pain. I felt like I was an enigma, in a class of my own, and not a class I wanted to be in. If the experts could not help me, what were my options in the future? I left the hospital at the end of August, having spent only five of the six to nine months that had been projected. A relief for me, but life became much more complicated as I integrated back into my daily routine and junior high school trying to find new ways to function with significantly less strength and chronic pain. I would have several trips back to the hospital to change and modify a series of casts that immobilized my neck for a year and my torso for almost three years.

My stay at the hospital was to have a profound effect on my life on multiple levels. My physical loss was obvious. Everything was harder to do and many abilities like raising my arms, swallowing easily, and standing for a pivotal transfer, were gone. In addition, however, and maybe even more importantly, there was also a change in how I viewed the world. I had entered the situation with the innocence of a child: relaxed, trusting, and optimistic. But the experience of a few months changed my belief system and introduced mistrust and fear of life, specifically of medical staff and of my body. I did not believe that the physicians had intentionally harmed me, but I did believe that for some strange reason they had not been able to truly see what I needed. In essence, this was a replay scenario of my initial bout with polio, when what should have been obvious medically was not and the results, horrific. It was as if they looked at me through a fun house mirror. No matter how hard they looked, their perception was distorted. And with distorted perception, how could the results be good? It would continue to be a common theme throughout the first half of my life, serving eventually as the catalyst to turn my attention inward towards metaphysics and healing.

I now did not trust my body's reactions. Suddenly, it had become unpredictable. All the effort to assure a good outcome had gone wrong even with the best of staff. My conclusions were that medical staff did not "get" me, and that my body obviously reacted differently from everyone else's, and certainly not in a good way. This helped form yet another conclusion: if my body was going to lose strength, then I would not waste a moment of "doing." I think I made a decision to take control. I was determined to do what I wanted to do, and not what I was afraid my body didn't want to do. I didn't realize that these new, dark beliefs about medical staff and my body would eventually have to be faced and released to avoid further crisis and suffering.

I also learned to turn off emotion to a much greater degree and literally tuned out my body to deal with the loss of function and pain. I took charge of my body mentally with a desire to control life, and learned to run two agendas simultaneously in my head: the first one that engaged me in all the activities of my non-disabled friends as a "normal" person, and the larger, second "behind the scenes" one that was filled with the extra duties and responsibilities of basic physical functioning on a daily basis with a disability, actions that most people take for granted.

I do believe now that the circumstances surrounding my onset of polio and my back surgery served to bring forth several major issues that my soul had come to earth to heal. I did not know anything formal at the time about metaphysics or spiritual awakening, so I used the only avenue I knew to create life: optimism, strong will, and sheer mental force. My mind had visions of a life similar to those around me who were not disabled, and I did not want my body to get in the way. So my will, focus, and drive became highly tuned over the next fifteen years to achieve the goals I set for myself. However, I believed I had to set my body's needs aside to achieve them. That would eventually catch up with me. Often times it is the toughest experiences that forge our character and that eventually turn us inward.

Chapter 5

Mobility in a Power Chair

There is pleasure if you know how to look.

School continued to be enjoyable, and I picked up a wonderful core group of friends through junior high and early high school. As the social scene during the adolescent years heated up, I could have been isolated because of my disability but that was not the case. For all of the things that were difficult in life, attracting good people to be with was not one of them. This was a supportive gift of Grace that came without conscious effort on my part. In some ways I was probably more comfortable with myself than most adolescents, since dealing with my physical issues took precedence over any interpersonal teenage drama, and my friends were not prone to drama, either.

Being good friends with someone like me entailed so much more than your average friendship that I could not have functioned well with superficial relationships. I had physical limitations and time constraints. I needed to be pushed from class to class. I could not do many of the activities that teenagers did, but I could talk. And because we genuinely talked about life and enjoyed each other's company, our friendships grew deeper, I believe, than most friendships at that age.

A simple teenage outing like shopping with friends, for example, was not an easy task. I had to be transferred into a car that could also hold my chair and be pushed while we shopped. Nevertheless, when my best friend, Carol, got her driver's license, she was excited to tackle the mall with me. Malls had just become popular, and it was a great way for me to shop at many stores without getting out of the car more than once. Carol borrowed her mother's Ford Galaxy 500 because its massive trunk was perfect to hold my manual chair as well as the lift that was used to get me in and out. She had the car, but most importantly, she had the desire and the determination to do whatever it took to get us there on our own. We felt so free, being off on our own, and had a great time. This shopping adventure was a prime example of the caliber of friends I had. Carol was not focused on the extra work it took to have me around, just the joy of our friendship. I was so fortunate to have friends like Carol who did not hesitate to responsibly offer their help to include me. Not surprisingly, I am still close to them to this day.

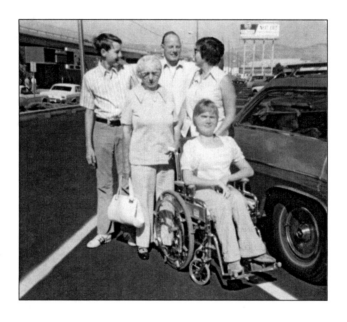

A family outing to Reno with my parents, my grandmother, and my brother.

The casting and bracing from my spinal fusion lasted through ninth grade. Life was full with the needs that go with that, and I was becoming more practiced in functioning with a much weaker body. I never liked asking for help, and this did not get easier as I got weaker. Life was busy for everyone in my family, and my grandmother, who had always been such a helpful, stable force for all of us, began her long road of dealing with Alzheimer's disease about this time. My needs had increased, and now the level of stress in my family began to increase as well with this added challenge. Gramma developed her own set of needs that became more intense and more debilitating over the next ten years. By the time I was in graduate school, I was helping her get dressed by verbally directing her, and driving her in my adapted van to my aunt and uncle's house for the day while I went to school and my parents worked. It was a reversed role of so many years, but it felt good to finally have the ability to help out for a change instead of always being the one who needed help.

My relatives were supportive of my grandmother, but the main responsibility was ours as we lived daily with her and her symptoms progressed. It was an emotionally intense time for all of us. Thank goodness we were a strong family because we all had a lot on our plate. Being in business for himself, my father had his own set of pressures. My brother had many responsibilities around the house by junior high as my grandmother changed. My mother continued to teach full-time, kept the house running, and was the family peacemaker. And in addition, they all had their daily roles in helping me. My independent nature, coupled with my reaction to the strained family dynamics, was to try to keep my needs to a minimum, or as minimum as I could get, since everyone was so stressed. I mention this here, this conscious choice to limit myself by not asking, because it was an essential belief that would need to change years later, not only to get my physical needs addressed reliably and comfortably through asking others, but also to open a channel to solicit and receive the flow of Grace, especially in difficult situations.

Although I mentioned earlier that I had no formal training in metaphysics or an awareness of spiritual awakening, I knew at an early age that there was more to life than what I could see with my physical eyes. Simply put, I knew there was a force for Good that I could direct through positive thought *that helped me move my body*. If I could not quite reach the faucet handle, for example, I took a breath, imagined and felt my hand reaching it, and it always gave me that extra inch of movement I needed to turn that water on. When I focused on exactly the movement I wanted, I got the best outcome every time. However, if my attention broke with even the slightest flash of doubt, my muscle strength immediately dropped enough that I would have to try again. These were finely graded energetic shifts that I probably would not have noticed if I had not been so weak. And since I was a child, I didn't question this mystery of life and over analyze it like adults tend to do. I was happy it worked and I didn't hesitate to use it. My weakness gave me the arena to experience this "I can" energy, and the effects were immediate and obvious. I did not know it at the time, but I was getting hands-on practice with the metaphysics of directing energy through affirmations, visualization, and intention setting.

As my time in high school grew to a close, my brother, friends and I set our sights on college and we were all accepted to San Jose State University (SJSU). We spoke about the usual concerns of getting classes and adjusting to college, but I had additional concerns to tackle. My brother and I would adjust our schedules each semester so I could get a ride to class (there was no such thing as paratransit services back then), but how could I get from class to class? My friends could no longer help since our schedules were so different. Power wheelchairs were heavy and bulky, and could not be put in a car. As I began to search for options, in came the wonderful synchronicity of Grace again. It just so happened that a new power chair had recently been developed that folded and was perfect for my needs. It was much more primitive than the ones available today, but it would do the trick! I was also introduced to an air-filled seat cushion that allowed me to sit for long periods of time without getting sore. This new mobility and seating presented itself precisely when I needed it, and was the beginning of a series of things that came much the same way over the next decade to bring me a high level of independence despite the severity of my disability.

Although I was thrilled with the idea of mobility in a power chair, I was not thrilled with the idea of actually *sitting* in one. I had sat in manual chairs for so many years that they became a part of who I was. Over the many years, I had built a subtle mental image of what "kind" of disabled person used a manual chair and what "kind" used a power chair and I definitely wanted to be in the manual chair category. In my mind, power chair meant more disabled. So even if I did not actually have the strength to move my chair for any real functional purpose, it fit the image. There was no logic to this image, but image defies logic sometimes. Intellectually, I knew that I needed to switch to a power chair to move ahead, but emotionally it was a challenge. During the first two or three weeks of college, I felt terribly awkward with my new image (the one, by the way, which was far more accurate for my level of disability) and felt sure everyone was staring at me and thinking I looked weird. Of course, no one was really looking at me that way. In fact, I probably looked more "normal" getting around on my own. It did not take long for me to acclimate to my new set of wheels. As I felt more comfortable, I felt freer. I often joked that once I was finally over myself, the freedom was so great that I'd have to be pried out with a crowbar to leave that chair!

Chapter 6

Finding My Vocation

When something has such divine purpose,
everything seems to open up without effort around it.

Some people search a lifetime to find their vocation, the career that divinely calls to them and, in turn, the one that feeds their soul. I was extremely fortunate to find mine right off the bat. I had a brief false start when I entered SJSU as a Behavioral Science major, but I soon was looking for something else. The memory of my encounter with the speech/language therapist on the playground in fifth grade, though present, had faded into the background of my mind. The universe reminded me, however, by bringing my attention to a therapist with polio who worked at Chandler Tripp School, a school for the orthopedically handicapped in the building where I still received therapy every week. The woman was physically stronger than I, but also used a wheelchair. I decided to observe her one day, and knew immediately that this was to be my profession. Communication was definitely my forte, and working with individuals and small groups at a table fit me physically to a tea. It blended my interests in education and health services, sparked by my own medical experiences and from stories and conversations with my family who were predominantly teachers and nurses. What a perfect match for me!

When something has such divine purpose, everything seems to open up without effort around it. San Jose State University happened to have an excellent undergraduate and graduate program in Speech Pathology. I signed up for classes that fall semester and was astonished the first day to find out that a new elevator had just been installed, literally two days before classes began, to the second floor where all the classes, therapy rooms, and audiological testing booths were located. No one had told me that there was no elevator, and I did not think to ask. Apparently, there had been no access previously to the program for wheelchair users. I did not miss the perfect timing of its arrival, feeling very grateful for that open door—literally!

The students in my classes were warm and interactive, and I felt immediately comfortable. I was right at home in classrooms full of verbal, organized, friendly, service-oriented students. During my time in undergraduate and graduate school, I was fortunate to have met many dynamic students who continue to be my friends and colleagues to this day, and to have been taught by an exceptionally diverse and competent teaching staff. High powered teachers, high powered students, all with a desire to serve the public to a very high standard. The coursework was rigorous, but I was grateful to be immersed in such a rich environment. The demands of the program brought us close together, and everyone's good nature added humor and fun socially to bond and enhance our interactions at many levels.

I had decided during this time to begin volunteering weekly at Chandler Tripp School in one of the classes for the orthopedically handicapped. My reason for volunteering was not what you might think. It was a good community service, but the primary reason was more about me: *I admitted to myself that I was uncomfortable around disabled people.* Now, you might think that was strange since my own disability was not exactly mild. However, I was not raised around others with disabilities and becoming an adult or being disabled myself had not automatically made me comfortable. When I saw the children leaving school each week as I went for my own occupational and physical therapy appointments, I was not as accepting as I wanted to be. How hypocritical, I thought, to be uncomfortable around disabilities when I had one, too! I also knew it was simply due to lack of experience on my part, and not about them. We often fear what we do not know so I decided to do something about it, to make a conscious effort to change my beliefs about who they were. I came to "know" them as people over the next three years, volunteering in a classroom of seven to ten year olds taught by two genuinely outstanding teachers. I helped with tutoring, feeding, and anything else that came along. I truly loved my time there, and I learned I could be responsible for my own perceptions and change the ones I did not like. My time with them served to dissolve an imaginary wall between us, the one I had created.

In addition to finding an outstanding training program in my own backyard, there was to be an additional educational gift of Grace that would give me expertise to offer in the workplace and help me compensate for any hesitations that might be directed toward me about hiring someone with such an obvious disability. It was 1980, and the realization that training was needed to address the needs of a rapidly growing, non-English speaking population had brought a grant to our graduate program just as I was entering. The extra course work and practical experiences working with clients in Spanish put us at the cutting-edge of the profession. I was quite grateful that my mother had insisted I continue taking Spanish through high school, often saying if I complained, "Lee Ann, you live in California. You are going to need it someday." Because of her belief, it became my minor in college. Little did I know that learning Spanish would open the door for me to become a specialist in this area.

Fortunately, I had an affinity for learning languages. Being raised in a bilingual, French household had helped. I understood French but did not speak it. Learning Spanish through classes all those years had given me some basic skills, more academic than conversational, but I was still barely fluent. I needed more language proficiency to be able to provide services, so I kept at it even though it was tough. Graduate school was challenging enough, especially with the additional needs of my body, and the one thing that had always been easy for me, listening and speaking, felt labored as I jumped into assessments and therapy utilizing my new professional knowledge through a language that was not mine. There were times I wondered what I was doing. Graduate school was hard enough in one language, let alone in two! The stress was high, but I knew it would be worth it in the long run. With persistence my Spanish developed and my professional knowledge deepened.

I am hovering above the earth with no body form, unlike my usual dreams where I am embodied and as disabled as when I am awake. I am looking down at Central and South America, noticing beautiful twinkling lights scattered throughout the region. I become aware of an energy next to me on my left, and I ask about the lights. "Those are places you have lived before," it said softly. "No wonder I speak Spanish and use it to help others in this lifetime!" I exclaimed.

This was a dream I had many years later, the kind of dream with exquisite detail that never fades with time, and allows a pearl of wisdom to float to the surface of our consciousness. The realization that Spanish was a natural part of who I am, and precisely why it had been used in my work with children in this lifetime, was eye opening. I was actually "remembering" how to speak as I worked, which would explain why I not only gained a good proficiency level without actually being immersed in it as most people do, but my accent was good. In fact, over the years I have had more than one Spanish-speaking parent ask where I had lived to learn my Spanish, wondering if it was somewhere in South America. Based on my dream, my Spanish could have reflected the accents of many countries.

Chapter 7

Discovering My Inner Slave Driver

*Looking back, it is amazing what my body was able to do,
and how forgiving it was in picking up after health issues,
trying to right itself towards health whenever I gave it a chance.
It held far more wisdom than I knew.*

Now that college was in place and my major set, it was time to find a way to extend my physical ability to better function in this physical world. I wanted to work and live independently. Two more pieces unfolded over the next few years to lead me strongly in that direction: a van I could drive and my first Service Dog, Isaac.

I cannot tell you how I knew it was time to drive, but the yearning to look into it became immense even though it seemed impossible. I could not transfer from my wheelchair, had no functional leg movement, and my upper body movement was quite limited. My grandmother did not see how it could be possible or safe and advised against it for all the obvious reasons. My mother, however, listened and eventually supported my efforts to look into it despite her own fears. She knew that determined look of mine, the one that is akin to placing blinders on a racehorse. I appreciate and respect to this day her willingness to support my decisions even if she worried. She had lots of practice over the years!

I had heard that Valley Medical Center nearby opened a new driver's evaluation program for the disabled. Converted vans with lifts and hand controls for driving had become more popular. I did not know if I had the strength to use the controls, and no idea how I would pay for it. Nevertheless, I had been persistent with my counselor through the Department of Rehabilitation about the need to drive in my profession and was finally referred for an evaluation. My muscle strength was evaluated, and I arrived several months later at the hospital for the driving evaluation. I was transferred into the demo vehicle, a sedan with sensitized power steering and hand controls, to see how I would do. I placed my hands on the full sized steering wheel and pulled with all my might, but it did not budge one inch. I tried again and again but with no better result. The evaluator, an occupational therapist, thought maybe there was something wrong with the steering. He reached over, and with one finger, turned the wheel effortlessly. My heart sank and a thousand thoughts ran through my mind. Was that it? How could I get to work if I did not drive? Did I have to give up and accept that I would never drive?

While I was seated in the vehicle and still swirling in thought, the evaluator mentioned another option. A gentleman in Southern California, Charlie Scott, had developed a revolutionary driving system, and the evaluator had scheduled my appointment on the day he would be in the area with a demo van in case I needed it. So it was back in my chair and off to the second part of the evaluation with hope again that something would work out.

Charlie was a delightfully kind man, an engineer by trade and past professor at UCLA, who had originally designed the driving system for a man too weak to use standard hand controls. What a difference! I could drive from my wheelchair, and there was remarkably no resistance turning the small steering wheel. It took little movement and little strength to move a two-ton vehicle. Perfect! The mirrors gave me full range of vision to compensate for my limited neck movement and everything else I needed to run the vehicle was closely located on a colorful, backlit button box. In those days, the extent of the driving evaluation in the van was a spin around the parking lot. They felt I was an appropriate candidate, and my persistence of more than two years with the Department of Rehab to authorize it paid off. The system was built, I spent a week in Southern California being fitted to it to meet my exact physical needs, and a couple of weeks later the van was delivered. It had come just in time. My brother was into his student teaching practicum and would soon be working full time, so rides to school were coming to a close.

Every night before falling asleep during those two weeks before the van arrived, I visualized the entire routine of entering the van, getting situated, and driving, in preparation for the actual driver's training. Somewhere I had read that the brain did not distinguish between thought about an event and the actual event, so I decided that I could get part of the training done ahead of time — anything to lessen the load on me physically. Besides, since visualization had always worked well for my body, it seemed natural to do as an extension of my body to the vehicle. It worked well, indeed, for I finished the actual driver's training in only a couple of weeks, less than half the time it could have taken, took the driving test, and passed. After the test I drove myself for the first time to SJSU for class. It was a little nerve racking to be completely on my own, but I relished the independence and overrode any fear about it. The song, "Ride Like the Wind" by Christopher Cross, blared on the radio as I drove down the expressway. "How appropriate," I mused. I felt free.

My mobility and independence now increased by leaps and bounds. Not only could I get to school, but the entire community was suddenly at my fingertips. Prior to the van, my excursions had always been limited. Transfers into a car were difficult and only allowed the use of a manual wheelchair, which by that point, was too heavy for me to push at all. If more than one stop was made, I stayed in the car. The power wheelchair and van, however, "leveled the playing field." They became a part of my body that gave me the movement to work and play that I'd never had before. They also afforded me the freedom to be by myself, something most of us don't think about unless we've been dependent upon someone else to move about. I liked my time alone, and being independently productive was empowering.

I was on a roll. All those years waiting for someone to move me were now over and I began moving physically and emotionally at a comparably higher speed. Having independent mobility allowed me to complete graduate school including semester practicums in a hospital and in a school setting. During the same time, I also volunteered as a speech assistant in the Disabled Students Program at San Jose City College. I wanted as much experience as possible before entering the workforce. I was going, going, going! Days were long. Just getting up and going to bed took a lot of time in addition to all the "normal" activities of life, but the effort was so worth it. I loved being able to do all of these things, knowing that with my disability life could have been so different.

I was grateful to drive, grateful to volunteer, grateful to be able to socialize with friends, and grateful to move. However, it was something that I had wanted so badly that with it came a fear of when it would end. Movement equaled happiness. Somewhere along the line I came to the conclusion that I only had a small window of opportunity to work and play like everyone else, and as my strength waned, the window would close and I'd be back to being stationary. That belief, based on fear, was entrenched in every cell of my body. This perception of lack about life, or limited Good, was a dominant perception that colored my decision-making for most of my adult life regarding how I treated my body.

I did not trust my body, a body that mysteriously lost strength. So the second conclusion that followed was this: If I just focused and forced my muscles to their edge at all times, I could make them perform to their highest capability for longer and literally squeeze more out of them. I truly believed that if I didn't use it I would lose it, and I was already losing. I was warned once that damaged nerves and muscles from polio died faster with consistent over-exertion, but I still held the belief from my back surgery days that my body did not react like anyone else's, and that I knew best. This inverted set of beliefs would cause me much suffering over the years as I weakened because I didn't see other options. Fortunately, after many years of

42

metaphysical intervention and studying, these beliefs were uprooted and replaced with a kinder, more healing set of truths, but not before I almost ran myself into the ground.

Some of my beliefs about life, like not trusting my body and ways to max out its movement, grew from interpreting experiences based upon one erroneous conclusion after another. Other beliefs just seemed to have always been with me, possibly from previous lives. For example, a feeling that I must use my will to force my muscles until there was not one ounce left (and I would simply drop) went unquestioned. It felt as though it were an issue of life or death. I can't even tell you what "drop" meant, except that there would be a long period of suffering with no relief and no one would be able to help. And most importantly, this path of suffering was the only way out of this body, so unavoidable. At my weakest point while still working full-time I remember literally feeling as if I would drop to the ground even though logically I knew that the rod in my spine and my wheelchair held me up.

These beliefs did not pop up at the time like a lit marquee to the forefront of my mind to be pondered for their relevance or validity. Rather, they subtly hovered at the edge of my conscious awareness, where they could permeate my thinking but not be confronted. Since then, I have revealed many such detrimental beliefs which I assumed were true about life, and discovered they were only beliefs, not law. It was not until many years of turning inward through meditation, reading, and metaphysical work that some light was shed upon them so that these beliefs could be more clearly defined and eventually released, to be replaced with truth about life. This kind of healing had to come from the inside out, like purifying water drop by drop with chlorine, to clear a path for higher level thinking. My egoic will was, and still can be, so strong that simply thinking with my mind about dealing with life's challenges caused more resistance and justification, evoking no lasting change towards a more peaceful state of existence.

Chapter 8

Isaac and Oak Grove

Isaac had a depth of soul that drew people to him. There was a presence and wisdom about him that people noticed as he looked in their eyes.

While in college I had heard of a program in Santa Rosa, California, that trained dogs for people with disabilities other than blindness. I loved dogs, especially golden retrievers, and was intrigued by the idea of partnering with a dog to help me do more on my own. I was concerned about adding more work for those around me with the responsibilities of an animal, yet the idea of having a dog to assist me and who would want to interact with me was exciting. I say "want" to interact because my experience had been that animals were usually interested in people who could physically play and interact more with them than I.

I immediately wanted to know more about the program, but found no listing through the operator. I then called the local center for independent living and asked if they knew of such a program. "No, but I will keep this note on my desk and if I come across something, I will let you know," the woman said politely. Believing the odds of that were about as high as winning the state lottery, I hung up and promptly forgot about it. One year later, a call came from out of the blue. "I have the phone number in Santa Rosa that you wanted," the woman said, as if I had just called her last week. I remember being shocked not only that she had found it, but also that she still had my number! I may have forgotten about the need for a dog, but the heavens had not. A pathway for the information I needed had been beautifully orchestrated and gracefully delivered on my behalf, making way for the first of three phenomenal canine partners that I would be blessed with over the next twenty-five years.

Three weeks after graduating with my master's degree in speech pathology, I drove to Canine Companions for Independence (CCI) to spend the next two weeks with a group of individuals also receiving their first service dog. I had found an accessible motel not far from CCI. Family and friends took turns staying and helping me with attendant care. Everything had to be well-planned to get my physical needs met so that I could focus my energy on the training.

The program was still in its infancy. They had purchased an old building for kenneling and training a small string of dogs. The faded green building was probably once a condemned chicken coop, but had been turned into a dog training center with dirt and plywood floors. A bale of hay in each kennel kept the dogs off the ground in case the roof leaked. The building may have been marginal, but it was obvious from the start that the trainers and dogs certainly were not.

We had each worked a variety of dogs the first two days but didn't know which dog we'd been matched with until the third day. We all held our breath in excited anticipation as the dogs were ceremoniously brought out, one by one, and the leash was given. Although we were not guaranteed our first choice, I had my fingers crossed for a reddish golden retriever named Isaac. There was something about him that just felt right. Needless to say, when they handed me Isaac's leash, I was thrilled! I had set my intention and focus strongly that morning for him to be the one. I thought that everyone else would want him, too. I was surprised to find out later that most, if not all of us, had received our first choice, which proved to me that it wasn't just about the dog or the person, but it was about the palpable chemistry between us that determined a good match.

We trained nonstop for two weeks outside in the summer's heat with barely a break for lunch. The training class was often referred to as "boot camp" for its intensity and straightforwardness. The trainers had volumes to teach us about handling and training dogs from a wheelchair and, in my case, how to do it well despite my very weak muscles. There was much to learn and perfect. Whatever we lacked in physical strength, we learned to make up for in emotional strength through clear intention, timing, consistency, and praise. We learned to be positive leaders.

Isaac and I at the motel where we stayed while participating in Team Training in Santa Rosa.

During the second week of training, Isaac and I had our first solo outing to a local hardware store. This was my first true test, to see if I could really handle this seventy-five pound dog alone. Although we had worked well in class, I had my concerns. This outing was in the real world, full of distractions and unexpected challenges. What if he jumped out of my van and ran away? I probably over compensated for my worries that day by directing him as strongly as I knew how. I should not have been worried, though. By the time we were done, I had a better feel for how gently he could be led. Isaac was a sensitive, deep soul of a dog. He responded well to my commands, and after getting to know him better as time went on, I realized that he honestly was more worried about my leaving him during that first trip than I was about him leaving me! It fact, we bonded to each other so quickly that I eventually nicknamed him

"Elmer," as in the glue. He was the most loyal, loving dog anyone could have ever wanted.

Isaac was a huge part of my life for the next ten years. We were always together and became partnered so closely that energetically, it felt as if we moved as one. We went to work together, we socialized with friends together, and we played at Lake Tahoe together. Of the many tasks that Isaac did for me, retrieving a multitude of dropped items and carrying my briefcase for work were probably the most helpful. There was also time for play, like hide-and-go-seek, or happily grabbing the ball even though I could barely throw it. No matter how much others played and interacted with him, Isaac constantly returned to his spot next to my chair, a position we were so comfortable with, doing life together.

Isaac had a depth of soul that drew people to him. There was a presence and wisdom about him that people noticed as he looked in their eyes. He often acted more human than canine, usually preferring to spend time with people rather than dogs. There was only one time that he was almost dog-like, feeling some sense of faint canine instinct, when he was given an over-toasted croissant that he promptly buried in the backyard. From that time on he sniffed the treasured spot whenever he passed by, in hopes of growing a croissant tree, I suspect.

For the first few years, if Isaac perceived a task as difficult, his less confident side showed and he would look up with those big brown eyes to quickly say, "I can't. How about you?" And each time I would wind him up with my voice, tell him he could do it, and wait him out until he was successful. That was always worth a big tail wag in the end, obviously proud that he had done a good job. With more successes came more confidence. If I were to describe Isaac's personality as a human, he would have been a tall, lanky intellectual with wire-rimmed glasses who enjoyed smoking a pipe while sitting on the couch reading the *Wall Street Journal*. More of a thinker than an athlete, a philosopher of sorts with a very soft heart.

The worries of taking on more responsibility and work by having a dog vanished quickly as we began our life together. My needs were met more fully than I ever imagined in a consistently happy golden retriever way. Isaac was a great help and fun to be with, and what I needed to give him was minuscule in comparison to what he gave me, as well as what he gave to others. One of the biggest unseen bonuses of being with Isaac in public was the positive reaction we suddenly received from people. The focus was now on the dog rather than my disability, and it softened the way people reacted to me. Often people feel awkward around people with disabilities, so they respond by averting their eye contact or by staring. I had become oblivious to it over the years, but my close friends were certainly bothered by the stares. Sometimes small children in their innocence would blurt out, "Look at that lady in the wheelchair!" A novelty from a child's perspective, but a comment often considered rude by their parent, so the children were usually reprimanded. Although they did not realize it, I believe this reaction unknowingly sent a message to the children that connecting with someone disabled was somehow bad. I remember, however, being quite surprised and pleased after Isaac's arrival when I noticed the children's comments change to, "Look at the dog!" which brought an immediate smile to child and parent. They often then approached us to meet Isaac, and in the process, met me as a person. The interactions were instantly transformed into a relaxed, feel-good exchange that benefited all.

Manned with my service dog, Isaac, independent mobility, and a master's degree, I was ready for work. As the first year of my temporary employment at the junior college was coming to a close, a friend told me of an opening for a bilingual speech/language therapist in her school district. I had been leaning more towards working with adults, but needed to find a job and thought the interview process would at least be good practice. In fact, I was not sure if I even wanted to work in the schools. I had heard horror stories of unreasonable caseloads, endless paperwork, and limited workspace. Since so many members of my family were educators, however, I decided to at least check into it. In my mind, I was just information gathering.

In retrospect, my non-attachment to the outcome was clearly of benefit because it allowed me to be relaxed, open, and be present during the interview. I am sure the interview committee, made up of administrators, a community liaison, and therapists, were a little shocked when I rolled in, dog and all. Nowhere on my resume had I mentioned, "Oh, and by the way, I happen to be extremely weak physically, use a power chair, and have a great dog!" Because of the interview process they would not be able to ask additional questions, but I am certain they had quite a few. I rolled up to the end of the long, boardroom table. As I was positioning my chair, I directed Isaac to his usual spot at my feet under the table. Everyone sat quietly with a polite smile and I sensed a bit of nervousness.

Suddenly, the woman to my right, who I later discovered would be my director, jumped in her seat. Isaac had decided to lick her knee before lying down, which understandably startled her, and which in turn caused the entire group to burst into laughter. Not perfect service dog behavior, but without a doubt, the perfect icebreaker. After the laughter and jokes quieted down, the interview proceeded smoothly. At the end, I chose to be straightforward with them about my muscle weakness, my strengths, and my need to understand the specifics of the job to help determine whether it was a good match physically. I did not want to get into a job I could not do, and I knew they did not want that either. I was offered the job a day or so later.

After touring the district and my main school site, I decided to take the job. And what I thought I might try for only a year turned into a spectacular twenty-year career as a bilingual speech/language therapist in the Oak Grove School District. For me it was a match made in heaven. The district had a warm, family feel from the administration down and my colleagues were top-notch professionals who worked together to serve children. I was impressed with their openness towards me and their willingness to see my abilities rather than my disability even before I had a chance to prove myself. I was fortunate that I had not met any of the obstacles of discrimination that many disabled people confront in finding and maintaining employment.

My work in Oak Grove was an enormous gift of Grace that appeared to fall in place before me with little direction on my part. It did not manifest through my conscious intention setting or affirmations, nor did I have to struggle before it appeared. It was so simply given, and true to many of the divine gifts we receive, that I had no idea at the time how far reaching it would be. I had a stable income, developed strong friendships, and felt valued by the staff and the community. And most importantly, the energy I felt when working with the students and staff made my soul soar. It brought in what I fondly refer to as "high octane fuel," giving my weak body amazing stamina to do as much or more than my able-bodied peers, and for many more years than I probably should have been able to do.

I literally rode on this level of energy for years, and with it also came an intuition that was clearly to help others. I became increasingly aware of an energetic feel, of sorts, between my students and me as we worked together. The more I learned and enjoyed the students and teachers, the more profound my insights became in assessing, remediating, and supporting student success. And as I learned over the years how to tune in and trust this intuition regarding others and myself, the more rapidly and completely my students improved. Over time I began requesting and using this inner guidance on a regular basis, which made immediate, visible, positive shifts in my students' sense of self and their learning beyond my expectations. Remembering to ask for divine direction in the moment, "What do I need to know?" with a challenging group of students, yielded some of the best spontaneous lessons and student behaviors that I've ever experienced. It helped in other work situations as well. For example, I learned that asking within for everyone's needs be met to our highest good, right before tough meetings, repeatedly brought about calmer, more creative solutions. The key seemed to be to *remember* to call in a deeper energy of wisdom to guide the way, and to focus on helping others from the heart rather than for egoic gratification. I learned to use that "high octane fuel" to elicit Good from my heart to directly serve others.

I had a Herculean job and I loved it. I spent half the week at my main school working with students in small groups and in the classroom. Driving my van throughout the district the rest of the week, I consulted with parents and staff, provided therapy and assessments for Spanish-speaking students preschool through junior high, and wrote a truckload of reports. I participated in, or led, committees and trained more than a dozen student teachers studying to be Speech Pathologists. There was even time to teach a class occasionally at SJSU. And if that wasn't enough, I often continued working in the summer to supplement my income. I cannot emphasize enough how much I loved working with the children, staff, and parents. Nothing has brought me more joy over such an expanse of time. The better I got, the more I was able to do, even as my body weakened.

This was the period of my life when I was at my peak for producing. I had acquired some essential elements for functioning independently over several years, and now they had finally come together. The framework was set to support my physical form, and my energy burst forward. No more waiting for others; I was off! It felt so freeing to not only move through my day by myself, but also to be able to contribute to society as well. I relished the fact that I had mobility, that I could go to work, and that I could socialize with friends and not be as dependent on them or my family. There was a time years earlier when my brother and friends began working as teenagers, that I honestly wondered if there would be anything I could do that would be truly helpful with a body like mine. I wanted to do something of value, but had no idea if I really could. I had finally found my niche.

Getting my body's daily basic needs met was a job itself, but there was never a doubt in my mind that going to work each day was invaluable for the sense of gratification that it brought. To do even the most basic of daily living skills, there was a full agenda, mental and physical, that ran simultaneously as I moved through the day alongside my able-bodied peers. The amount of energy, time, and focus to do both "jobs" was enormous, but not overwhelming. I had learned self-discipline and persistence early on and accepted the extra work as part of life.

Although I had achieved a great level of independence during the day, I was not independent enough for any physical self-care. Now you would think with all the personal physical help I had received since infancy that I would have been comfortable with asking and receiving help. Not so! I wanted to do things by myself as much as possible and hated asking for anything more than I absolutely needed. Since physical self-care was time consuming, I kept my needs to a minimum even if it wasn't healthy so that I had more time to do what I wanted. For me, that meant sitting all day and completing tasks slowly but steadily with determined focus, being organized, and even restricting water intake so I did not go to the bathroom all day.

Chapter 9

Juggling a Multitude of Balls on One Foot

But it was clear to me that I could not, and would not, be held back by fear.

The final big step on my roll toward independence was to live on my own. Several years earlier I had met a disabled couple who lived and worked independently. Both had post-polio and used power wheelchairs, and with their adapted house, attendants, and basic equipment, they lived a happy, productive life despite significant physical challenges. They were great role models for me. So I set my sights on saving to buy and adapt my own home as soon as I began working. Renting an apartment, even if it was adapted, was not an option to meet my physical needs. I essentially needed a house to be "fitted" to my high level of disability so it could provide me a stable base from which to function, and I needed it for a reasonable price.

This was a huge undertaking, but I was not to be deterred. Fortunately, this was where my trait of stubborn persistence was unquestionably beneficial in disciplining my thoughts to focus on exactly what I wanted without wavering. The more I heard well-meaning people tell me their concerns regarding safety, finances, and finding dependable help when I'd mentioned my plan of moving out, the more adamant I became that I could do it. My family was understandably worried, but supportive. I told myself that I could not be the only disabled person in Santa Clara County who lived independently with my level of disability. Basically, I did not want to be told no. I was fully aware of those fearful "what ifs"; I felt them myself. But it was clear to me that I could not, and would not, be held back by fear. I remember thinking how mad I would be if I looked back someday and found out that it had just been fear that stopped me, nothing more. I was feeling a deep longing to live on my own, and my longing and focused attention were greatly met by Grace to guide my way. My responsibility in this endeavor was to hold firm that it was, indeed, possible.

I had read somewhere that directing intentional thought energy for manifesting one's desires was enhanced by writing down the desired outcome and visualizing/affirming it daily. A relatively novel concept in 1986, but somehow I had picked it up. I had so many physical limitations for making things happen in life that it was exciting to me to consider this other avenue that, for me, had no restrictions. Having saved for four years while working and while living at my parents', I finally had a down payment and was ready to start seriously searching for a house. I had been looking in the paper on a regular basis for a couple of years as if I were ready to buy, so I had a pretty good idea of what I wanted and the price ranges. I had written down a detailed list of "have to have's" and "would be nice's," the optimum features that I was looking for in a house. I gave my realtor a copy of the list and asked him to keep his eye out for me. I was in no hurry and was willing to wait for just the right house.

My parents and my brother wanted me to find something close to their neighborhoods so they could be available if I needed them, but I did not think I could afford it. Looking at the prices in the paper, I thought I would have to make do in areas that were less expensive and farther away. Over the next two months the realtor called me regarding a few houses in my price range, but they were not what I was looking for. I really thought it would take close to a year to find a house that would work since I had such specific needs. Waiting also gave me more time to save money and, truthfully, would bide me more time to be ready to tackle living on my own.

One day my mother convinced me to drive through a nearby neighborhood to see what was for sale. Although I reminded her that I could not afford those houses on my beginning teacher's salary, she was open to looking and I figured I would just go along with it for her sake. So much for thinking I was doing *her* the favor, and that finding a house was still a far away venture! We wrote down several addresses, gave them to the realtor, and were able to see one of them right away. The house was perfect. It had been on the market for three months (coincidentally the same amount of time that he'd had my list), and although he did not understand why it had not already sold, the sellers had just dropped the price into my price range. Bingo! Even more impressively, as I looked at the house I was amazed to see that it had all the details on my list as if I had seen the house before writing them down.

Now it was time to do what I had been talking about for four years—it was time to make the move to live away from home. What I thought would take a year had only taken three months, so ready or not, here it was! I purchased the house and spent the next several months getting some basic renovations completed. I had unexpectedly been asked to teach a couple of classes that year at SJSU, not knowing that it would be the extra money I needed to get the house ready. It was a well built, but neglected, twenty-eight year-old home. There were ramps to build, usable door handles to install, flooring changes to be made, wall switches to be lowered, a garage door and opener to be replaced, and the list went on, including a vast amount of cleanup inside and out that was taken on by my brother. Although I had no previous experience in adapting houses, I'd had plenty of practice problem solving in other areas of my life so this project felt natural. I wasn't looking for anything fancy, just functional, and I had gotten good at being functional. The modified bathroom was my biggest and costliest challenge. I knew I needed a roll-in shower, but did not know if the area was large enough. That had been divinely provided as well, when my contractor pointed out that removing a hall closet behind the shower offered us plenty of room. My parents paid for the bathroom modification, and I was on my way.

Some people might say this house was just great luck, but the manner in which everything was so consistently provided to perfection beyond any of my own expectations was clearly a gift of Grace. I had definitely set my intention and affirmed it regularly, but I could not have brought about this kind of result with my own energy alone. The outcome had been magnified a thousand-fold. I felt so fortunate to have been brought to this house and was grateful for the pathway that made it a reality. Having lived in this home for the past twenty years, I have come to realize the great stability it has afforded me so that I may go out and do life. For the first time, I had independent access out of all doors in the house, access to water, a freezer and microwave I could reach, remote lamps and lights I could turn on, covered access from my van when it rained, blinds with a long wand that I could open and close, and a roll-in shower. I continue to appreciate the ability to shower with relative ease, as opposed to the many years of struggling to transfer from a bathtub. I joke that it took me 28 years to take a shower, but it was a serious relief to simplify something so basic to good health and comfortable living.

Living on my own also meant finding a way to get my personal daily living needs met and being able to pay for them. Most people think that with my level of disability, there is a magical funding source to pay for personal care attendants from some magical agency. This has not been my experience. I made an appointment with the Department of Social Services but was told that I did not qualify for supplemental government assistance because my $19,000 a year income was too high. When I asked how people like me lived independently, the clerk suggested some group homes for the disabled. Although that is a viable solution for some, it was not for me. I told the clerk that I had not gotten a Master's degree to live in a group home, and I left determined to find a solution.

I solved the problem by finding roommates, often college students, who lived with me rent-free in exchange for helping with personal needs and household chores. I had a structured schedule for the two roommates and myself so that the hours and responsibilities were clearly defined between work and non-work. This arrangement was generally successful for about six years, though I often felt like a den mother settling differences between roommates and stressing over finding replacements so that my home and care were stable. It served its purpose financially, but when changes or problems occurred with one roommate or the other, it disrupted my stability as well as the dynamics of the household. Not realizing it was time to create something different, I struggled the last year or more finding suitable help. With several changes in one year and more drama than I cared to live with, I was at my wits end.

I was anxious about life and emotionally drained, not knowing what to do. It was obvious that the latest roommate situation was not working out and the thought of going on the hunt yet again was overwhelming. I needed a whole new system, though I did not know it. Since all of my affirmations, visualizations, and persistence were attempts to recreate my current set-up rather than something new, the results became less effective.

It is Saturday morning and I am sitting in my backyard swirling in thought about my attendant care needs. I know I need direction, that I am missing something important. To calm my frantic thoughts, I find myself repeating, "What do I need to know? What do I need to know?" I desperately need a twinkle of insight to enter and offer some clarity. Suddenly, I am awash with the most profound, unshakable sense of peace and my entire body relaxes. Simultaneously, a thought gently enters my mind: "You need to separate who you live with from who takes care of you." I am instantly flooded with understanding: I know it will heal old emotional patterns from childhood; I know it will create new stability; I understand the purpose of my recent struggles. I feel calm and without worry, for I know its Truth. I am completely at peace.

I had no words for this experience but I knew its source. I had needed divine guidance and it had burst through, significantly changing my life for the better. With it also had come an actual physical response, a deep sense of unshakable calmness, which helped me hold on to its reality. The Presence had felt wise, loving, strong, and kind. I had such a deep sense of certainty and peace that any concerns about finding hourly attendant care or paying for it vanished. I was sure the change had already been made even though I did not know how the specifics would play out. I did not have to convince myself that I'd be okay. I knew it.

This state of peaceful certainty lasted for several weeks. I began looking for help, found my attendant care within only two weeks, and my roommates moved out. For the first time in my life, my dog Isaac and I were alone at night. Not the safest situation when you cannot move, but I pushed all fears surrounding it away because I knew that making this change would bring peace to my home. I was alone for over a month, and other than praying that my aides would indeed show up to get me in and out of bed (which they did), I felt free. Though I enjoyed the solitude, I began looking for a roommate to help financially and provide someone at night in case of an emergency. My previous student teacher needed a place to live, so that fell into place beautifully, too. Although finances were tight, I visualized unlimited checks in my checkbook to cover the bills, and I always had sufficient funds. I didn't try to analyze how it was happening; I was just thankful that it was happening.

Out of all the challenges of living with a significant physical disability, finding and maintaining good, reliable attendant care has been the one that continually tests my trust in life. Thank goodness for my parents and friends, especially in the early years, who bailed me out on more than one occasion when I needed help. Since I have never been able to get in and out of my chair, dress, bathroom, bathe, or prepare food myself, I have had to have my primary needs met daily through the hands of others. It is most personal and is essential to all other activities of life. When these needs are not met, an immediate solution has to be found. I've needed to trust that I will always find someone to help each time an attendant leaves even if fear tells me otherwise. My personal needs, which cannot be set aside for even a day and which increase over time, seem rigidly set forever while on this earth. However, the way they are met is changeable and repeatedly makes life feel uncertain. It has been on my shoulders to individually find, train, manage, and pay my attendants regardless of whether I am well or not. It has driven me to manage life from a broader, metaphysical perspective in order to find relief and a sense of peace, and that has been the invaluable silver lining in an otherwise potentially dark cloud. It has brought me a practical, conscious partnership with the Divine as I have sought the wise, kind flow of Grace to do what has often seemed impossible. It has been as significant a force as the physical traumas and illnesses in moving me inward to strengthen an intimate connection to the Infinite for receiving Grace.

Having unstable attendant care is like juggling a multitude of balls on one foot. It takes much more energy to coordinate the extensive details of the day when I feel off balance. The fear of not finding consistent help for these basic daily living needs, and the changeable nature of staffing over time, triggers a primal instinct for survival that has the potential to be more paralyzing than physical paralysis. It has unquestionably caused periods of my greatest stress, but it has also honed my skills by repeatedly directing my intention towards Good to find what I need in a healthy way and not give in to fear.

I suppose one of the other benefits of handling the stress of getting such basic needs met is that it makes all other stresses of life at work or with others seem small in comparison. It puts things into perspective. For me it clearly separates "needs" from "wants," and reminds me to be grateful for all the little things, and for all the wonderful women who have worked with me over the years. Their care allows me to do life on my own every day. The more I awaken and learn to exist upon inner wisdom for creating and guiding my life in a calm, Grace-filled way, the more stable and peaceful my attendant care has become.

My twenties had definitely been the decade for physical manifestation, putting the essential pieces in place so that I could move into independent adulthood. I had seen that using my thoughts in a positive way through clear intention setting, affirmations, and visualization repeatedly brought forth what I needed in a magnificent way. I remember at the time telling a friend how powerful it was, feeling quite proud of what I had discovered and a little too cocky about my part in it. After telling her how I had directed my thoughts so successfully to create what I needed, she gently smiled and commented, "Well, I believe that is God giving to you, not just you." Undaunted, I was quick to say, "Yes, but I did it," as if she didn't get it. At that time in my spiritual development, the Divine still felt far away and, therefore, I believed I had to work intensely to bring pieces of Its goodness to me. I did not feel that base of a steady, already-given Grace that I have come to feel and exist upon more today. I knew the manifestations were high-level divine energy at work, but I was taking way too much credit for my part of the process!

I believe I had been experiencing wonderful third chakra creations, from that solar plexus level of energy that the ego directs. It was the best way I knew at that time, with laser-like focus, to find what I needed, to take charge, and to try to direct life. This thinking, dominated by the ego, remained fear-based, however, with a strong but subtle suggestion of lack. It implied that if something "bad" happened that I had somehow been at fault, that focusing harder with my will could force an outcome my way, that I had to direct everything myself through unending thought and focus, and most importantly, that I knew best. I had not yet developed knowledge or trust in divine order, or in asking and surrendering outcomes to a greater wisdom for good. I believed I had to diligently control and direct all the little details of life. And based on that kind of thinking, it is not surprising that life eventually presented me with so many serious "details" that I could not control them all as my body spiraled downward. I had to find help that worked, something "out of the box." The next two decades brought me into a deeper realm of the metaphysical in this quest for help, through books and through several phenomenal women who taught and healed me metaphysically as I learned to work on myself from the inside out.

Chapter 10

Breathe in Life

My resolve became stronger and stronger with each success, and the universe powerfully rushed in to meet my expectations.

By the age of thirty, I had been living independently for two years and working excessively for six. My mind loved it, but my body did not. I noticed I had lost strength a bit more rapidly throughout my body than I had in childhood, including more weakness in breathing at night and general swallowing. However, it was subtle, like sand slowly draining from an hourglass. I held a diffuse set of beliefs surrounding my disability that losing strength, struggling more, and a decreasing quality of life were inevitable and unchangeable. Therefore, I reaffirmed somewhere along the line— even more adamantly— that if I could not stop the weakening, I would take charge and use to its maximum every ounce of strength that I did have before it, too, disappeared. There was so much I wanted to do and no time or strength to waste.

I was thirty years old and had never had a clear medical diagnosis, just the descriptive labels from Stanford when I was four. So I decided to have a neurological exam to confirm that these difficulties, especially those relating to my weakening throat area, were indeed related to my disability and not to something else. The exam was uncomfortable to say the least as high levels of electric current were run through my different muscle sets to look at their responsiveness, but I finally received a clear diagnosis.

"You have had polio," the neurologist said, "no doubt about it." He was surprised that something so obvious had been missed. I was actually relieved to finally have a definitive diagnosis after thirty years of being an enigma to the medical field. I had not gone to the neurologist looking for a solution that would rid me of my disability. I was looking for a reason for all the physical issues, something that tied them together and made some sense. I had been concerned that my swallowing weaknesses could have been due to something unrelated to the original illness, like a tumor. I now had a diagnosis, a label I could wrap my painful experiences around. It not only validated how serious the initial illness had been, but also validated for me that the multiple, related difficulties I had accumulated over the years were significant and not just in my head.

I felt "satisfied" with the results, though they did not explain my steady, lifetime weakening. A pearl of medical wisdom regarding long-term loss would emerge intuitively years later. For now, just the confirmation that I was dealing with polio and the experience of being "seen" medically was progress.

I had been told once by someone with post-polio that my muscle strength was like burning a candle, so I should not force my movements or the "flame" would burn faster and run out sooner. It was meant as a kind warning to consider moderation, but that did not suit my personality. My philosophy was not to hold back, and I was okay with burning the candle quickly if it meant I was free to do what I wanted.

Though I was not outwardly prone to anger, I will now say that this stance on life was at least partially fueled by hidden resentment regarding the medical atrocities I had experienced that had not only been painful but had made daily movement so much more effortful. This emotion fired me up to move through life, luckily, rather than spiraling me down. It served its purpose for many years to get me mechanically through quite a few tough situations, but eventually I had to learn to use it with more wisdom and in moderation, in order to bring peace to my mind and body.

This aspect of how I approached life was not very Grace-filled, but thank goodness it did not spill out to darken my interactions with others in an angry way. The kindness that was so easy for me to give to others was hardest to give to myself.

Years later I would uncover a similar belief that had gone unrecognized all of my life but that had underscored all of my decision-making regarding how I treated my body. Fueled by an unconscious, gnawing fear of suffering, I believed I had to push my muscles at all times, not allowing them to relax for fear they would not pick up again. In my mind, strength meant quality of life, and quality meant an independent lifestyle similar to my able-bodied peers despite my disability. I focused on keeping a maximum output by "keeping the bar raised" in pushing what I could do even as my body balked. Since I'd had a pattern of growing weaker physically, I also believed that eventually when I could not force my body any longer, I'd somehow be done with the ability to help others, which had felt good, and be left to deal exclusively with the worse aspects of my body. I'm not even sure what "done" meant, but it felt very dark. I had an unquestionable fear that long-term physical suffering would be unavoidable once I was "done" and before I could die. How ironic that when I finally did have to stop forcing my body because I was so overwhelmingly depleted at forty-five years old, a gateway miraculously opened to shift me more rapidly toward the Divine rather than spiraling me downward into a suffering, hellish state. What had been held so firmly in fear was ultimately met and released by a tidal wave of Grace.

And so I often drove my body relentlessly, a slave driver of sorts, not believing or recognizing any wisdom in the messages it gave through its health or lack of it. The weaker it got, the harder I pushed. I argued with it constantly, until I could argue no more, and only then would I finally make a change and do things differently in order to back off from some of the emotional and physical strain. I now feel that this belief—that I had to push myself to the point of exhaustion in order to survive—had been built over many lifetimes, based on the depth of its hold and its subtle yet wide-spread influence on my thinking. It sounds, I'm sure, unbelievable that I would actually think this way, but it was deeply ingrained and unquestionably real to me. I thought this approach to my life was an unavoidable fact because of my disability. I believed I had no choice but force if I wanted to live well and avoid physical suffering for as long as possible, though in reality it was the very thing that caused emotional and physical suffering. Looking back, it is amazing what my body was able to do, and how forgiving it was in picking up after health issues, trying to right itself towards better health whenever I gave it a chance. It held far more wisdom than I knew.

Not until many years later, after a profoundly frightening experience, did a new set of thoughts surface that shed light on the old — allowing the belief in resisting my body and therefore, my life — to be quietly released and eventually replaced with a more gentle belief seated in the infinite wisdom of knowing and experiencing the unlimited possibilities of the universe.

It is Friday evening and I am leaving the emergency room, having been seriously misdiagnosed once again. The kernel of corn, lodged in my throat for almost a week, hovers dangerously near my windpipe. I am told by a physician that my case is not an emergency, that my airway is not currently occluded. My pleas are not heard. "Come back Monday if it's still a problem," he mutters as he walks coldly out of the room. The nurse tries to reason with him on my behalf, but to no avail. There is no logic to this scene, only the recurring theme of not being "seen" correctly. My body is panicked for its survival. I feel scared, angry, isolated, and a deep sadness engulfs me. Exhausted with seemingly no option again, I suddenly have a quiet, unwavering thought as I cross the parking lot to my van. "You cannot address your body from the outside. You must do life from the inside out." Its message resonates with clarity and truth. I begin to relax. I am given hope again.

In an instant I was transformed by this powerful, dynamic thought with which I felt profoundly aligned. It came out of the blue, obviously not of my own thinking. This was another pivotal point, more significant than all the others before it, to turn my attention inward. I am tempted to say that this was the answer I'd been praying for, but that would be only partially true. It was the answer, but its wisdom was so far beyond the scope of my limited thinking that I did not have the thought to pray for it, nor did I understand how profound it was at the time. It did provide me another concrete example, however, that we are carried by Grace. I was not alone in dealing with my body, for the Heavens were completely attuned to the details of my plight and already had the best solution. My job, I would be taught over and over again, was to remember to ask for and listen to Divine Insight first and foremost, and thus my thoughts could be infused with Wisdom. Then, and only then, could I begin to move in a direction and truly trust that the rest would unfold to my greatest good.

Two days after leaving the emergency room, the dreaded kernel of corn finally passed without incident. As I was rolled on my side to get dressed that morning, I happened to roll a bit father than usual and felt the obstruction move a bit. I immediately told my aide, and her knowledge as an occupational therapist came to the rescue. She gave me some ice to chew and swallow while still in that position. Its coldness helped my weak swallowing muscles contract to move the food gently through, and my throat was finally clear for the first time in seven days. It left rather humbly; its purpose had been served. The message had been received loud and clear. No longer did it need to stay as the signpost to direct my focus inward for healing.

This was not the first time I'd had a serious issue with food and choking. About six years earlier, a piece of lettuce closed off my airway completely. Luckily, my brother and mother had been home. By lifting me out of my chair and onto my side, the lettuce fell partially aside so air could pass for temporary relief. However, true to my theme, I was not correctly "seen" in the emergency room when I arrived by ambulance even with all the conscious directing and focusing I could metaphysically muster for a calm outcome. I was sent away from the hospital with the obstruction still present.

Feeling the lettuce flipping on and off my windpipe, I knew I could not go home or I would die. So my parents and my aunt (Aunt Jo, once again) drove me to the county hospital where a young intern agreed that something was wrong. After more than an hour of working down my throat, he finally pulled out the quarter-sized piece of lettuce. His creativity in working down my throat and his phenomenal persistence solved the problem without the further dangers of surgery. My calm outcome had finally come.

From that point on, however, I continued to have trouble with food sticking in the same part of my throat for several days at a time. I reasoned that if I chewed carefully, its size would not be life threatening when it stuck and this gave me some semblance of relief emotionally. Though I did not want to feel fear about choking, it always loomed in the background of my mind as a potential danger.

I will say that dealing with medical nightmares like these taught me over the years how to become calmly powerful in moments of crisis by being intensely present. There is such a natural force for Good that comes through us and others when we become present, and once it is experienced, there is no mistaking its Truth. I had repeated practice with medical crises to immediately let go of all thought except for those aligned with what I wanted, and to hold steadfast to those thoughts moment by moment until a more peaceful result arrived. Eventually I learned to expand this skill deeper within me, to hold open a pathway with thought energy that allows this sacred healing energy of Grace to come forth for miraculous results. The more I could become present and hold this pathway open from my heart without having to control all the details out of fear, the more relaxed I became and the greater the result. I was learning to use my will for, I believe, its true purpose: to hold my thoughts on a positive outcome despite what I saw with my physical eyes or what I feared from past experience instead of using my will to direct and control every detail. My medical experiences would become too serious to control it all; I needed to let go into something bigger. I was learning how to surrender, to literally get myself out of the way so that a greater, wiser force for good could lead. And with each experience over the next two decades, I became more comfortable in trusting Its lead.

I knew I did not want to live anymore with a fear of choking to death, so the week after the hospital incident, I decided to get counseling to help deal with the fear. Counseling seemed to align itself with the insight I had received regarding addressing life from the inside out. I was not one to just jump into looking at emotion, but any resistance was countered by the need to lessen my fear of choking. A friend of mine had been sharing her experiences with me about a therapist she'd been seeing by the name of Mary who, I thought, had an intriguing way of looking at life. What caught my attention was the concept that health issues were not random, but reflected unconscious emotional issues that needed to be addressed for a body to move towards health. What a concept! I knew for a fact there was a mind-body connection in directing my body, but it never occurred to me that my body was actually trying to *say* something. This idea is more widely accepted now, but at the time, it was revolutionary. It was just what I needed. It would be out of searching for solutions to the darkness of multiple, serious health issues over the next twenty years that old patterns of thought were broken and my greatest spiritual growth obtained.

Mary soon became my therapist, too. She coincidentally had been a nurse before becoming a therapist, the perfect blend of experience for me. I worked with her over the next two years, learning to become aware of life and its messages through my body's health. Mary was the first professional to offer me real assistance in beginning to deal effectively with my body in an entirely new way. Although our sessions were not dominated by all things metaphysical, I was drawn to anything she mentioned related to energy, thought, the body, and healing.

Mary began by introducing me to some basic metaphysical principles regarding emotional thought and its effect on the body. I'd had plenty of experience using positive thought to maximize my body's functioning, but I had never touched upon facing negative thought. I was an expert, actually, at diligently avoiding negative thought because I was well aware of how detrimental it was to my muscle movement. However, avoiding it, I'd discover, did not mean it was absent or that it was not affecting my body. Within the first few sessions, Mary posed a question relating to my choking problems that stirred my thinking. "You can cut off a leg and live, you can cut off an arm and live, but you cannot cut off your throat and live. What is your need to cut off your airway? What are the thoughts behind it that your body is reflecting?" Not knowing the answer to her question, she recommended I do some journal writing to gain insight into what choking symbolically meant to me. She probably had no idea how essential this question was, but it was incredibly on target in leading me to pinpoint the problem that quickly resulted in better swallowing.

Journal writing for guidance proved extremely effective for me. By the next session, I had my answer. As I wrote it became clear that choking symbolized flashes of death. Steady weakening had felt, I realized, like a slow, physical death with a body that I believed would continue to go awry. Although I was a positive person and wanted to make the best of it, I thought I had no option but to do "misery" as it came and be strong. And as a result, part of me wanted life to go quickly in order to avoid sustained suffering, though another part of me knew I was not one to give up easily. The result was a conflict of thoughts that was erupting through my throat. I had to look honestly at my beliefs if I wanted a chance to lessen future suffering. I did not know they were simply beliefs that had permeated all of my perceptions; I assumed they were just facts of life. Always quietly undefined but significantly present, these thoughts had been supported by my repeated experiences of finding nothing here on this earth to help — not physically, anyway.

Once these beliefs were brought more directly to my attention, I knew that they existed as thoughts and that thoughts could be changed to create something better. It was a call to consciously wake up and develop my thought energy to a higher level, or frequency, to support a very damaged body. I had no clue that this was actually a spiritual call, to fine tune through physical experience my awareness of and gratitude toward, Grace. It was calling me, to move toward and exist upon the higher, more pure realms that provide gentleness to a body, wisdom, true peace, and joy in all aspects of life. It was a serious call, a guide for soul development, while in this physical form.

With these realizations, I could now question, "Suffering and death. Is that what I want? Is there another option?" The opposite of death was life, so I made up my mind to take charge of opening my airway from the inside out by affirming a new direction, "Breathe in Life." I now had a new approach. Instead of trying to clear my throat physically, I'd pause as soon as I felt food stick, take a gentle breath to relax, and tell my body calmly but firmly to breathe in Life. Simultaneously, I'd visualize the inside of my throat lined with a slick, smooth surface and the food slipping down properly. No more struggles, no more using a physical response to correct a physical problem. I employed instead an energetic response directed through thought to correct the physical problem, and the results were nothing short of miraculous. Within a month, I noticed that obstructions passed more quickly and soon they were occurring less often. After six months, food lodging in my throat became a rarity. Now my careful chewing and swallowing were effective, and if something small did stick, I had an effective way to help it along.

This was the first time that I'd been so successful in improving a physical condition with my body that, by standard medical thinking, could not be done. In fact, my swallowing could only get worse when viewed from a purely physical perspective. I'd received a medical evaluation before beginning my work with Mary. Two swallowing evaluations and video X-ray footage had shown documented, concrete evidence that I should not have been swallowing food well at all. I had little if any muscle contraction for swallowing, and "pocketing" on the right side of my throat from lack of muscle tone where the food had been lodging. The recommendation was to grind all solid food. That, however, was not something I was ready to consider.

Regaining my ability to swallow more safely through a metaphysical approach was an empowering breath of fresh air, literally. If I'd had any doubt about a direct correlation between my thoughts, emotions, and my body's response, they were whisked away by such rapid, miraculous results. The seriousness of the problem kept me highly motivated to insist upon nothing less than clear, safe swallowing and breathing. Life, or death, no wavering. My resolve became stronger and stronger with each success, and the universe powerfully rushed in to meet my expectations. I had found a gateway to direct and support my energetic field, a field inextricably influenced by my thoughts and emotions, the field upon which my physical form rests. I knew it worked because I'd experienced the change myself. And with anything rooted in the Divine, the presence is so solid that there is no question of its reality. It is only doubt itself that pulls us away from our access to the Divine.

This completely changed my perspective on dealing with my body. Previously when I'd have trouble physically, I'd think, "Oh, not that, too!" as if it were unrelated to whatever was going on, or had gone on, in my life. The awareness that it was *telling* me about life, a help rather than a hindrance, was brilliant! I did not know that this was to be the catalyst for deepening my spiritual knowledge. I just wanted relief from fear and pain. And just because my body was "talking" did not automatically make me want to hear what it had to say! On the contrary, I was good at arguing with my body, and continued to be until just a few years ago when I had no strength left with which to argue. Over the years the serious need to find solutions related to my disability, when there seemed to be none in sight, has pulled me gently up a divine energetic spectrum that I have learned to call forth and exist upon for support despite outward, superficial appearances. I have found that sometimes wisdom presents itself but we have to grow in order to fully receive its benefits.

My swallowing muscles had not significantly improved, but my *functioning* had mysteriously improved and that's all that mattered. I did not need to question its reality through logical thinking. I was experiencing the results. Since then I do not put such limits on functioning or outcomes based on what I see. What I think sometimes is real based on physical perception isn't always what it seems. There is so much more that can happen, thank God!

I now had an insatiable drive to read anything I could get my hands on relating to energy, health, and soul development. Bookstores had begun carrying small sections of books on these topics that have since grown by leaps and bounds. I had never had an interest in reading before (I preferred "doing" over sitting still and reading), but all of a sudden I was so thirsty for knowledge that I was like a sponge. There was an excitement about learning, a deep desire that I'd never felt before. My soul was probably dancing! I had finally been turned in the right direction. I read books by Louise Hay, Thomas Moore, Marianne Williamson, James Redfield, Eva Pierrokos, Gary Zukav, Barbara Brennan, Shakti Gawain, and Doreen Virtue to name a few. I also read, *A Course in Miracles*, which profoundly shifted my thinking and brought me a solid sense of peace about life.

I began seeing common threads of information in my reading that rang true about my body based on past experiences. Everything I read about perceiving life's events in a deeper way for improving health and for getting needs met made so much sense to me. My medical experiences were interwoven signposts for my soul development towards higher truth, not just fragmented disasters with no hope for change. I remember thinking how much formal education I'd had in thirty years, but how little I knew about the essence of life. I needed to go beyond a physical, concrete level of looking at life to a metaphysical, abstract level for my soul to soar and to flourish despite all my body's difficulties.

I was fascinated by the idea that events and our reactions to them actually pointed toward subconscious thought patterns dominating our inner world and manifesting in our outer world. I was desperately in need of some inner wisdom to handle my body's health and day-to-day functioning, to gain an understanding of my body at a deeper level that could give life instead of drain it. I'd eventually come to realize that my disability had been the perfect instrument for learning, even though at the time, I still had no trust in doctors or my body.

I started questioning physical cause/ physical effect, and began looking at my body through an energetic cause/physical effect paradigm. Barbara Brennan's books, *Hands of Light* and *Light Emerging*, accelerated my knowledge in this area. No other reading had tied together the divine energetic interrelationship among the physical, mental, emotional, and spiritual bodies for me as completely as hers. It resonated through my entire being as essential knowledge for healing at all levels.

I wanted to maximize whatever physical strength I had so I could work and drive as long as possible, and metaphysics definitely seemed like a promising avenue. I used its principles to drive my body towards what I wanted, not what I didn't want, with a long-term goal of squeezing out every ounce of function from my body before it stopped moving completely.

Now there was another belief to question, the belief that I had to gather and use up all of my strength while it was around because there wasn't enough for my lifetime. I saw myself as responsible for accessing this divine energy for good, like a commodity, to use as best I could. I still felt too separate from It, but supported in many ways by It. I believed I had to work hard to capture pieces of Grace that came from someplace far away. That was my level of knowledge at the time, which was more than I'd ever known before but small in comparison to where I am now. I had not yet learned to relax and ask for Divine help that brings with it an even greater amount of blessings. Years later I would move closer to that level of understanding and finally *feel* the Divine love and wisdom that this energy carries, bringing steadfast peace and joy. But for now, I plodded along trying to educate myself on the essence that carries life.

Chapter 11

Finding More Support

My experience with Jan gave me another tangible example of how willingly and powerfully the universe rushes in to support our well being even when given only the slightest opening to enter.

My life remained busy and fulfilling, and though I had limited movement, my stamina seemed endless. I had plenty of energy to be on the go all day and usually returned home right before going to bed. With my power chair, adapted van, and service dog, Isaac, I moved steadily throughout the day until 8:30 p.m. when my hour routine of getting to bed began. Some people might be bothered by living with such a rigid time schedule to begin and end their day, but for me the schedule gave stability and predictability in getting basic physical needs met. With these needs met, I could go out and create life.

Even though I used a lot of energy for daily living, I also had the energy to "play." This changed in later years when my energy waned, but at that time I enjoyed having fun. I liked anything outside, especially regional parks and mountains. "Rolling around" on dirt while being in nature was one of my favorite pastimes. I eventually discovered that what I was really sensing and enjoying in these outings was the divine energy of the earth. No wonder it felt so good. It fed my body and my soul. I had many friends from high school and college so movies, dinners, and shopping always seemed to be on the calendar.

Many of my friends had wonderfully creative senses of humor. They certainly had not forgotten their child side when it came to relaxing and socializing. There were the theme birthday parties, like my 30th when everyone arrived dressed as old ladies, and not pretty ones at that! They left nothing undone, bringing suitable attire for me to wear as well and creating games relating to geriatric themes. You can only imagine what the gifts were like! Then there was the "Dessert of the Month Club," comprised of a small group of us from work who loved sweets and good conversation, and who met monthly wherever good desserts and coffee were served. It was our job to look for new places to meet and socialize, following our motto of "Search and Serve It." Since we all worked in some aspect of special education, our motto was a silly twist to the special education decree to "search and serve" students with special needs. It was an enjoyable way to relax after a long day at work. And do I dare admit to the annual reindeer run, when we would sneak onto friends' front yards at night during the Christmas season to place inflatable reindeer on the front lawn, complete with strategically placed piles of chocolate covered raisins? My job, since I could not move about inconspicuously, was the driver of the delivery vehicle. You never knew where those reindeer were going to show up from year to year, and sometimes they landed back in my own yard! This kind of silliness was a great balance to the often more serious side of life.

My body had been amazingly accommodating for many years, but around the time I was addressing my swallowing problems, I began having my first experiences with kidney stones and infections. One of the reasons I had more flexibility and time to get things done was due to my decision since seventh grade not go to the bathroom all day. Yes, *all* day. That meant I waited from 5:30 a.m. until 8:30 p.m. by limiting my water intake and by sheer will power. Though I knew it wasn't the healthiest decision, I was willing to put my body on hold to lessen the demands of the day. It made life simpler when I was younger, and as an adult, I did not see how I could work and be tied to going home mid-day since I could not be transferred in public restrooms. Finding the personnel and finances to take care of myself seemed like another roadblock, so my solution was to detour it completely for as long as I could. It would take me until my late thirties to begin weaving in a bathroom break after work each day. Thank goodness I'd had enough experiences by then, both painful and peaceful, to slowly move me in a direction of finding the willingness to give myself more support and to trust that I could find this support.

This was my first severe kidney infection, and it led me, finally, to a doctor who was supportive and helpful. My trust in dealing with my body through doctors was at an all time low, but my confidence in directing my body through affirmations and intention setting was high. I'd had a urinary tract problem all week but I did not believe I'd get accurate medical help. I wanted to be able to take care of my body myself. However, my relationship with the medical world needed healing, and so I would not be allowed to go it alone. I didn't know it, but I was about to meet my new permanent health care professional.

By Saturday I was so ill that I knew I had to do something differently. As a last resort, I finally drove myself to the emergency room with what I thought were kidney stones and the flu. And by the grace of God, the urologist on call was not only personable and experienced, but seemed genuinely interested in listening to what I had to say about my body before deciding the course of action. Although I was very ill, I recognized that the universe was bringing me a doctor who was truly helpful. My inner search to find a more stable way to support my body was actually beginning to spill out into the physical world. Hallelujah!

I was relieved at his decision to have me stay in the hospital for a couple of days, because I knew I was too ill and too weak to go home. Feeling as though I'd correctly been "seen" for once by the medical community was tremendously healing, as was something that the doctor told me during my follow-up appointment a week later. Looking at me squarely, he said, "You were very ill by the time I saw you in the hospital. I am sorry I didn't listen to you over the phone and treat you sooner, but I didn't know you or your case." The night before going to the emergency room I had called the office of a urologist I had seen once in hopes of getting an antibiotic. The doctor on-call, who turned out to be this emergency room doctor, was honest in saying he could not blindly treat me over the phone, but that he could be of help if I landed in emergency. He had been straight up with me, and I understood and respected his position. His interactions and interventions once I did see him in emergency had been so right on that I thought he should be commended, not apologize. His genuineness and compassion made me appreciate him even more. It also somehow seemed to soften some of the emotional scars from the many previous medical disasters, something he was totally unaware of I am sure. His honesty, kindness, and obvious ability to "see me clearly" was astonishing. He gave me hope that my medical needs could be met without such suffering. Luckily, he was not afraid to take me on as a permanent patient either, and continues to be my doctor to this day.

Although I'd had much success affirming and directing my body to keep up with my busy schedule (notice its purpose was to support my schedule, not my health), I could not consciously create a physically stronger one. I told a friend one day that my arms and shoulders felt like weighted sandbags and that it was making movement even more difficult. Even though I didn't say it directly, the thoughts that surrounded that statement related to a fear of dealing with more physical decline. In fact there was a lot back then that I didn't say about fear and functioning even to myself. I was worried that if I admitted something was scary I might not be able to do it, so I would avoid the emotion altogether and plow through with logic and will.

A conversation ensued regarding doing something about my weakness. "Why don't you get some physical therapy?" my friend asked. Having experienced weekly therapy through early adulthood and still having lost strength despite it, I didn't believe therapy would change anything. I had all my justifications for why it was hopeless. I told her that my muscles didn't strengthen like regular muscles and there was nothing I could do about it. And besides, I explained, insurance didn't pay for therapy to address a long-term disability and I could not afford to pay privately. Those seemed to be obvious dead-ends to me. But what I also didn't mention was my belief that even the slightest strengthening would serve only to prolong an inevitable decline and struggle, not reverse it. I did not think it was possible to weaken physically and feel good. I had never questioned these thoughts because I was convinced they were real and unchangeable, but something in the interaction between us that day allowed me to step back slightly and observe them for once a little differently. Through my friend's questions that day, a ray of light entered and I found myself suddenly willing to look for some relief. I decided to try getting massages to see if they could release the heavy, stagnant feeling in my muscles.

Mary, my therapist, gave me the name of a massage therapist she had seen at a chiropractic center near my house. I made my first appointment with the massage therapist, Jan, and felt immediately comfortable with her and her ability to work on my muscles. The massages were helpful, but I had been sent to Jan for an even bigger intervention. She'd recently had such a profound healing of her own damaged knee from a method of soft tissue manipulation called Structural Integration, or Rolfing, that she was enrolling in a program to become a Rolfer herself. She offered to work on me at home when she was done with her training to help develop her skills. Normally, I would have been hesitant to try something new for fear my body would not react well, but surprisingly I felt no resistance.

Jan became the second phenomenal woman in my thirties whose intuition and skills as a Rolfer made the next important shift in healing my unconscious belief system about supporting my body. She was a natural, and was obviously intuitive in working gently with my muscle sets. Damaged muscles and severe osteoporosis would not be where most people would want to begin learning, but Jan was calmly unafraid. Her first session with me had an immediate, profound effect. Even though my spine is significantly curved, I remember sitting up and for the first time in many years feeling balanced and straight. The heaviness in my arms, shoulders, and neck vanished, never to return like that again. I felt stronger and realized I had a new sensation physically, one that was not pushing against what felt like an energy of resistance. After the ten session series, I felt well balanced, and the energy and strength I now felt seemed to flow more freely through my body.

My experience with Jan was like a heavy burden had been physically lifted from my neck, shoulders, and arms. As I write this, I can't help but wonder whether it was those burdensome beliefs about my body that had held so much weight, straining a very sensitive physical form. A release of a layer of those beliefs rippled through my body and lightened the load on many levels. Later on this concept of releasing limited or fearful beliefs and emotions regarding my body was key in releasing supplies of energy to my muscle sets for extended years of movement. It takes energy to hold suppressed emotions, and I needed to free up all the energy I could get.

Helping myself had been easier in many other aspects of my life, thank goodness, but was clearly a major challenge when dealing directly with my health. My experience with Jan gave me another tangible example of how willingly and powerfully the universe rushes in to support our well being even when given only the slightest opening to enter. I initiated its entrance by having a sincere willingness to do something to help myself, but even that willingness was not purely of my own doing. It had been opened to possibility by Grace during the conversation with my friend and pointed me in a better direction. Once I made the decision to do something, the rest unfolded to become a much deeper form of support and healing than I could have ever planned or executed on my own. My part was to act on it.

Chapter 12

Saying Goodbye, Saying Hello

I had become aware by then that unwanted emotions often blasted through my body like a freight train, so I set aside my stubbornness to force an agenda and decided to lie down and rest...

I was noticing that Isaac, my service dog, was slowing down. Although his entire being still centered around our life together, he was now ten years old and having to work harder at daily tasks. Unlike a pet that can spend much of its day resting, Isaac was used to being "on." He had an automatic alert system, ready to move or perform a task at any time. Even while he slept under my desk at work, Isaac's attention was never fully detached as he listened for the click of my motorized chair. Though his general health was good, his stamina and physical strength were weakening with age. Movements like jumping up with his paws against counters in public to handle money exchanges, standing quickly to move alongside the chair, or just being on the go throughout the day obviously took more effort. Jumping into my van with the briefcase in his mouth was also becoming a struggle, so I adjusted by having him stand on the vehicle's lift and raising or lowering it so he could just step in and out without straining. It was quite a sight multiple times a day, rain or shine, to get the "handi" (my term for "handicapped") dog in position to help his handi owner.

As deeply devoted as he was, Isaac would have never asked for a change in duties. His heart had not changed, but his body had. Though the thought of retiring him was difficult, I did not want to force his body or drive him into the ground. Had I not been willing to make a change, he would have done his best to please me for that

85

was all he knew. Thank goodness I had some sense about taking care of his body even if I had little sense for taking care of mine. I knew it was in his best interest to retire him even if we didn't like it, and to create a new kind of relationship where we could spend time together without taxing his body. I was fortunate that my parents had recently retired and lived close by. He would be well loved and cared for there, and I could see him regularly.

Isaac was such a superior partner that the next dog had awfully big paws to fill. Knowing my busy lifestyle and the extensive manner in which I used my dog, CCI was very sensitive in finding and training a dog with the potential to meet my needs. A trainer came one day to video tape Isaac at work and watch our interactions, and I was invited to work a few preliminary dogs to better determine placement when it was time. I was willing to participate in anything that would make for the best pairing, so before Isaac retired, I spent the day with the exceptional trainers at CCI working with a few potential dogs.

Since I did not have the strength to drive myself to Santa Rosa and back in one day, my parents transferred me into their car and off we went, about a two and a half hour drive. I remember gazing out the window at the beautiful, green, springtime hills along the way as I grappled with thoughts of taking in a new dog. I hoped that if I was okay with retiring Isaac, that somehow he'd be okay with it, too. As I sat with these thoughts and a desire to make this transition well, I slowly became aware that my heart felt walled off with resistance. Noticing this was a big realization for me, as at that time, I was not practiced in recognizing my feelings. How unfair it would be, I thought, to shut out a new canine soul looking for a partnership. I knew I did not want to receive a new dog that summer with a closed heart.

The movement of the car and the sight of the hills are mesmerizing. "I do not want a closed heart, but how do I open it?" I find myself thinking. Suddenly, I am in front of large castle doors latched solidly shut. I want to know what is behind these wooden doors. They begin to open slowly. I am surprised to see a beautiful, female golden retriever standing on the other side. Her golden fur shines as she looks at me expectantly.

This experience was so out of my normal realm of thinking that I knew it was significant. I had learned by now that life was full of signs, and that this brief vision was meant for guidance. I probably should not have been surprised, then, when the last dog I worked that day at CCI was a beautiful, blonde, female golden retriever named Zinkle. She was high energy, interested in everything, and so full of life. She definitely needed more handling than I was used to, but she obviously had the drive to be a great worker. I knew it would ultimately be the trainers' decision as to the final placement in a few months, but luckily they asked for my input. Had I not had the vision, I would have said my preference was one of the other dogs, the male golden who seemed low key and easy like Isaac. However, I trusted that the vision was not just my imagination but was clear guidance, and I told them that Miss Zinkle would be my first choice. She was so completely different from Isaac in every way, and I wanted a difference so I would be less likely to compare dogs. I would not know for several months whom I would be paired with, but I was comfortable waiting, and I left.

Isaac worked his last school year in 1993, retiring when he was eleven and a half years old. At the end of the school year, I attended the district's annual Recognition Dinner where employees are honored for specific years of service and for retirement. Unbeknownst to me, Isaac had been included in the list of district retirees, with nine years of service to the district. When his name was called for recognition of service and retirement, Isaac received a standing ovation. These were his human friends from all over the district, having visited with them each week in his gentleman-like fashion as we traveled from school to school. Isaac was led up to receive a certificate and a ceramic treats jar. He took the certificate in his mouth, wagged his tail, and brought it back to me. He was not quite sure what all the commotion was about, but he knew it was good.

I handed the leash to my brother that July to take care of Isaac while I was in training. I drove to Santa Rosa, heavy hearted but focused on the excitement of getting another dog. Isaac could never be replaced, but I had made room in my heart for another. The training lasted three weeks this time and a documentary narrated by actress Betty White, a devoted dog lover, was being filmed during team training as well. I was pleased to be placed with Zinkle after the first few days, and the long days of training with the others began.

My brother brought Isaac to visit several times during training so he would not feel so left out. Isaac knew something was up, and had been very melancholy as soon as I left. Nothing seemed to make him happy, and it was clear that he intuitively understood that we were separating. It was hard, to say the least, for all of us to see him so sad even though we knew it was the right thing for both of us. I held firm that if I could just feel good about the transition, Isaac would follow my lead. I don't know that I truly felt good, but I spent a lot of energy telling myself that I did. I thought I had to be strong to carry both of us emotionally. I never admitted to myself how hard the transition was, but Isaac certainly had not been fooled.

The first time Isaac met Zinkle was near the pool at the motel where we were staying during training. I had no idea how it would go. I knew aggression wouldn't be a problem because of their sweet dispositions, but what I really wanted was for Isaac to like her. Would he see her and feel even more displaced? Would his feelings be hurt? All worries vanished as they met. I swear it was as if they already knew each other. Isaac walked up, licked Zinkle's nose, and stood near the chair. No big fanfare, no climactic scene, just a relieved dog who was happy to be back in the mix. Isaac completely accepted Zinkle without an ounce of jealousy. I believe he thought our family had simply expanded and that we would be functioning as a threesome.

I was glad that the dogs had come together so easily during those early meetings because things had been a little more challenging in the "Let's get to know Zinkle" department. She was highly motivated and effervescent about experiencing life. Her daily schedule, though, had been turned upside down for team training and the unpredictability wound her up beyond her usual exuberant self. She was also unsettled by this shift in leadership. Getting into a new, stable routine would help immensely later on once we were home, but for now Zinkle was highly stimulated and seemed to focus on everything and everyone except for me. I could see that her potential was tremendous as I watched her work with her trainer, however. When she joined with him, she was focused and flawless at every command, a model service dog.

Trying to harness her level of energy and direct her effectively when I had not yet earned a position as leader in her mind kept me on my toes. We needed time to bond so that I would stand out to her in the crowd, so to speak, and broaden her field of awareness from a "me" to a "we" perspective. But that was going to take some time. So in her eagerness during training, Zinkle managed to knock a cup of hot chocolate down my bare leg and into my once-white sneaker, pulled my arm behind me as she unexpectedly took off to join the other teams leaving the movie theater, and swallowed my movie ticket. Yep, one gulp. Thank goodness she was eager to work, affectionate, and happy which helped balance the many "Oh, no!" experiences!

The stronger our bond became, the more incredible we were as a working team. Zinkle turned into a powerful worker and loyal friend. She was confident, fun, and eager to please. In fact, once I learned how to work with her, she was an incredibly quick, intuitive learner. She seemed to understand the purpose of tasks and was self motivated in completing them correctly. Zinkle soon exceeded the working level that Isaac had obtained and continued to learn many new commands over the years to help support me as my physical needs increased. The trainer had been right. She was a breeze to work with, and learned an incredible sixty-five commands in her time with me.

I was amazed at Zinkle's interest and ability to so effectively communicate with humans. She was clearly here to engage in the world, no doubt about it! I got my first dose of her intellect and level of engagement one evening at the motel during training. I noticed Zinkle wasn't in the main part of the room, so I looked in the kitchenette area. She had been so very quiet that I was a little afraid of what she might be up to. To my surprise, she was standing excitedly next to the table with a look of great anticipation. At first I didn't get it, so I asked her what she was doing since she was clearly not going to budge. She pranced a little in place to get my attention and then glanced up at the table. It was apparent that she was trying to tell me something, but I still wasn't quite getting it. I think I was a bit shocked that a dog was trying to direct my thoughts instead of me directing hers! So she pranced and glanced at the table a couple of more times, patiently waiting for me to get up to speed. All of a sudden I realized she was trying to direct my attention to the box of dog treats in the middle of the table. "Are you saying you want a dog treat?" I blurted out in disbelief. She let out a large "woof!" as if to say, "Yes, Lee Ann, that's it!" She was relieved, I'm sure, that I wasn't quite as dense as I looked. Needless to say, she got her treat and I got my first training from a developed soul cast in a dog's body.

This type of two-way communication between us became more and more refined. The more vocabulary she learned, the more she could engage in the human world, or maybe I should say the more I could engage in hers. I was used to having a dog who watched more passively for his part in the interactions of the day and who looked to me for direction. Zinkle, however, was an initiator and used thought and body language to express herself at a very high level. The better I got at reading her, the more that channel opened for spontaneous communication and the deeper our connection became. It was partly telepathic and partly verbal, and often allowed us to do tasks in the moment that had not been previously practiced. She was a sponge for vocabulary, but beyond that, her brilliance and intuition allowed her to link word meaning for new comprehension. She was incredible.

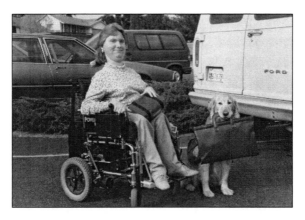

One of the many stops with Zinkle on my travel days in the district.

Not only was her working ability a good match for me, but also her fun-loving personality was a good balance to my more serious side. Nothing seemed to faze her or disrupt her happiness. If I found the need to verbally reprimand her, she'd flash a brief sign of remorse, and then look up and wag her tail as if to say, "Are you over it yet?" She was as enthusiastic about work as play, and needed play time regularly to burn off energy so she'd be in a better space to inhibit impulses while she worked. Her need for play ensured that I had playtime, too, and gave a breather to my driven personality. There were occasional play dates with other service dogs, and regular walks to satisfy her canine need for some "olfactory rush" time as well as my human need for quieting my mind. She helped the teachers de-stress at work as well, playing hide-and-go seek or racing after the ball down the hallway after school. Zinkle shared her healthy perspective on life with all of us.

Isaac lived with my parents for the next two years. Because he had worked for so long, he was not accustomed to staying home, and it was important to keep him feeling useful. He learned new routines with my parents, like riding in the car to buy the paper each morning and carrying it in the house. Since he was used to being at school, Isaac made regular trips to spend the day in my brother's fifth grade class. I saw Isaac many times a week, and often took him to work with Zinkle and me on Fridays when we stayed at one site. He loved his trips to work to visit his friends, both adult and child, and loved lying in the room that had always been his. Since both dogs knew how to work with me, there was no difficulty on my part handling them despite my weak body. They waited their turn for directions, Isaac carrying the lighter soft lunch box by the handle into work as Zinkle wielded the more cumbersome briefcase. Isaac would watch as Zinkle did her job, generally content now with his new role.

And then one day the inevitable happened; it was time for Isaac to say goodbye. He had been weakening steadily and had not felt well for several months from relentless intestinal problems. He was thirteen years old, and I had decided long ago that I did not want to lengthen any physical suffering if I could help it. So when I felt it was time, which probably was a month or two longer than I should have waited, I left work mid-day and my parents and I took Isaac into the vet and let him go peacefully. I was clear that it was the right thing to do, as was the vet, but our hearts were heavy. Mixed in with the grief, though, was a sense of relief that Isaac would soon be set free. He marched into the office with surprising strength, and if I didn't know him better, I would have thought I'd made a mistake. There was no doubt in my mind that he knew, too, that it was his time to move on and he was ready. He did not share our human emotion of grief and loss to physical death. I do think he was relieved. The thought of the transition, I believe, gave him strength.

Isaac had seen me through my quest for physical independence and watched me begin my inner journey toward deepening spiritually and supporting my body. His job was done. I did not go back to work after the appointment, which I would have normally done in the past no matter what was going on. I had become aware by then that unwanted emotions often blasted through my body like a freight train, so I set aside my stubbornness to force an agenda and decided to lie down and rest after our goodbyes.

I am in a cul-de-sac on the front lawn with my neighbor standing to my left. Suddenly from my far left, Isaac and Zinkle come bursting forth, shoulder to shoulder, running together like a team of horses. We watch as they race with incredible power, joy, and freedom, running straight and then curving to the right. They are together in perfect step, moving as one. "Wow, look at them go!" my neighbor exclaims. "Yes," I say, "didn't you know? We just let Isaac go today."

This was my dream as I fell asleep that afternoon. It gave me such peace to see him strong and happy again. He really was set free. I thought it was significant that he ran so perfectly in sync with Zinkle. Maybe it was to symbolize that the space he had held in his union with me had expanded and was well supported by her. He was leaving me in good hands.

Chapter 13

Miraculous Solutions, Fast

I began asking the heavens to hold me safely out of my body...

The sessions I received from Jan supported me with a more even flow of energy through my body that relaxed my muscles and freed up some additional physical movement to use over the next few years. That was good since I needed all I could get. I was still slowly losing strength, but Jan's work helped me to be far more functional than I would have been on my own. Zinkle was high energy and fun, the perfect partner for my on-the-go lifestyle. We were so closely paired that I believe her happy, strong energy flooded my own energy field and added to my stamina.

I found myself making some small changes to accommodate my strength level. I spent a little more time at home, which had become a peaceful place with attendants who did not live-in. One of my teaching friends moved in as a roommate about a year into the new attendant set up which helped create a calmer, more stable atmosphere. I also stopped doing private assessments for other districts but continued a wealth of other responsibilities in addition to my regular job. I took a break from working during the summer for a few years, but eventually had the opportunity to create and teach a summer class for Speech Pathology students participating in a bilingual training grant at SJSU. I loved that, too, and continued to teach the class for many summers.

My main job paid the monthly bills and my extra jobs allowed small improvements to my house each year. In the back of my mind, there was the ever-present feeling that my window of physical movement was slowly closing. I did not know how I would support myself or do anything to the house once I became too weak to work, so I continued to push my body and energy with my will to do as much as I could, while I still could.

I continued to read books relating to metaphysics and spiritual development. As I read, I saw common threads of information that rang true to me about life experiences, thought, emotion, and intention setting. I practiced and practiced directing my thought energy more purposefully and with greater detail to improve outcomes for my body and general functioning. I could see that using this energetic process for creating my life yielded far better results than would normally be expected. I was becoming more aware of the interconnectedness of life and how richly symbolic life experiences were in divinely guiding my development.

Though I was gaining a more direct, conscious alignment with divine energy to gently support me, life still was fast-paced and often stressful for a body with little movement and a mind that did not want to be limited by its lack of movement. I have never really "seen" my physical weakness accurately, which has been like a double-edged sword. It has allowed me to energize and ride on my strengths, but at the same time has created a huge gap between what I thought I could push myself to do and what my body could realistically provide. The weaker I got, the harder I pushed. By the time I was almost forty, there was a tremendous amount to organize and coordinate just to do the day, and I felt stressed. All the pieces of my day, done through others or with special equipment, had to line up perfectly and do their part for my busy schedule to run smoothly. And just like a line of dominoes, when one piece fell, it knocked out others.

Simply attending to my daily needs kept me on my toes. The juggling of attendants, schedules, and what to do if they were suddenly sick and could not come, was always present even with the most reliable of help. My wheelchair and adapted van had to be kept in perfect working order at all times, as literal extensions of my own physical movement. And my body, which was usually last on the list for my attention, began to gain my attention by having more difficulties. Although my stamina was still very strong, I was starting to have difficulty overriding my body's needs in pursuit of the life I wanted. I still believed it was completely on my shoulders to control and direct life by using energetic intention and will. In other words, I saw myself as egoically in charge, but with an avenue to elicit divine help to enhance the various details that I attempted to control. So much so, in fact, that I soon became hyper-vigilant to "hold my life together" stemming from an array of beliefs that emanated from fear. This eventually became an impossible feat due to the sheer number of details I needed to address on a regular basis.

I had a couple of surgeries around this time, one of which was an emergency appendectomy. I knew something was seriously wrong that day but could not pinpoint it. For some reason, I did not yet have severe abdominal pain. My body felt bloated and anxious, and I remember saying that I felt like I was ready to pop. My doctor recommended that I go to emergency, and though I resisted it, my brother fortunately talked me into going and took me in. Not knowing where this was headed but afraid that it could get quite complicated and dangerous medically for me, I immediately set my thoughts in motion to ask for and hold the possibility of clear divine guidance and intervention—fast! I needed the doctors to see clearly to diagnose the problem and find a way to address it without causing more trauma. I did not want any more fragmented, dark, medical experiences, so I was adamant and intensely focused on asking and directing my thoughts in hopes of a favorable outcome. As the hospital staff attempted to diagnose the problem, I continued to pray for them to be guided. I decided my best bet was to ask the divine energies around me to talk to the divine energies around them to get it straight and just skip the whole human thing altogether!

All the usual challenges began to present themselves. My body was so stressed that neither my veins nor a major artery would accept the multiple attempts to insert a tube intravenously. By now the doctor knew I needed surgery right away but I was still without an I.V., and intubation (placing a tube in my airway) for anesthesia with such weak breathing and swallowing muscles was risky business. I knew my body would heal well from surgery, but I was afraid that my airway could become permanently impaired if I were intubated. Although there appeared to be many dead ends, my focus did not shift. I knew the outcome would be influenced in my favor regardless of the problem if I did not waiver and continued to work from the inside out.

I needed some miraculous solutions. Just as everything seemed to build up to one, big, impossible dead end, the solutions finally appeared, one after another. The surgeon on call was a delightfully competent, humorous, insightful listener who was courageous enough to attempt something unconventional for this unconventional patient. I asked him if there were any way to do the surgery using sedatives instead of general anesthesia to avoid the risk of intubation. Though he had never tried it, he thought it could work if they added injections of local anesthesia to the site. Good answer, I thought, as I finally felt myself relax a tad. Remembering a part in one of Barbara Brennan's books where she describes "seeing" patients being lifted and held above their bodies by divine energies during surgery, I began asking the heavens to hold me safely out of my body, too. This, I thought, would make me less likely to react to pain as they worked and help keep me from needing general anesthesia.

As I was being rushed to surgery, a familiar face suddenly joined the race with me to the operating room. "I can't believe it's you!" he exclaimed with an incredulous look on his face. "What are the odds that I would be on call?" There stood the anesthesiologist who had just helped me several months earlier by using sedatives instead of general anesthesia for a kidney stone procedure! I was so relieved to see him. He was exactly who I needed. "I know. I need you," I replied, as I quietly thanked Grace for sending him. "They could not get an I.V. in yet." I continued, "You were able to do it for me before, so could you do it again, please?"

I now had the perfect surgeon, the perfect anesthesiologist, and the gang on the other side to hold me away from pain and direct the show towards a positive outcome while I was asleep. Now I could let go. He inserted the I.V. in one shot, and my next memory was of waking up after surgery with a sore belly but independent breathing. The surgeon said I had done amazingly well. He was obviously very pleased and I'm sure relieved with the outcome. Needless to say, so was I. I could relax knowing my breathing and swallowing had not been jeopardized, and I had no doubt that my body would heal quickly. During my follow up visit, the surgeon was still commenting on how amazing the whole experience had been and that my case had been the talk of the town among his colleagues. He thought I was pretty amazing, but I just smiled because I knew it had been so much more than just me. The same anesthesiologist was divinely sent again a couple of years later for a foot surgery. To say that he was shocked to see me again would be an understatement. He actually seemed a bit shaken by the synchronicity of our meetings, but I was simply pleased and grateful!

My experience with having an appendectomy was a huge step for me in spontaneously blending the metaphysical world with the physical world to create a safer and healthier outcome for my body. I applied everything I had learned up to that point about directly engaging and aligning myself with that strong, divine energy that heals, and the results were miraculous. The all-too-familiar dead ends and potential for trauma had loomed in the distance, but never manifested. Something unquestionably had changed. The pattern had been broken. Instead of being a constricting, painful experience, this had been an expanding, healing one. Once again, that power for good had come through the medical hands of others to successfully help my body. What a profound experience to begin a healing that was three-fold: a healing of my body, my emotions, and my beliefs about getting help medically.

One evening a couple of years later I decided to surf the Internet, something I was not accustomed to doing. One thing led to another, and I eventually landed on a site advertising a weekend conference on metaphysics and alternative health in San Francisco. Only in retrospect did I see that this was another profound pivotal event, the kind that changes the trajectory of your life's path forever. Divine guidance was floating in to begin my next phase of spiritual awakening and healing. The thoughts that guided me that day did not come rolling in like thunder to get my attention, but arrived softly, immediately sparking my interest. It was that feel of excitement and interest that should have been a clue as to how perfect this conference was to be for me.

I do not remember who the speakers were except for Dr. Barbara Brennan. I had recently finished reading her two books, *Hands of Light* and *Light Emerging*, so her name caught my eye. I decided to register my mother and me for one of the conference days. I selected a variety of presenters as our first, second, and third choices, knowing that we might not see the same presenters if the classes were full. When the registration papers arrived, I was surprised to see that, not only did my mother and I get the same classes for the day, but also they were all with Barbara Brennan. At first I wondered if I was missing out on something by not getting to see the other presenters. Fortunately, I decided to let it go. I had learned by now to be more open about synchronicity and divine order, and was willing to believe that there was a reason for such a schedule to occur for both of us. I was not disappointed.

In her two classes, Barbara not only talked about the human energy field and health, but also demonstrated an energy healing on a woman with a severely sprained ankle. I watched as she worked using the energy from her hands to repair the lines of energy (my interpretation) running through and around the damaged area. When she was done, it was obvious that the woman's pain was significantly less. Everything I read in Dr. Brennan's books had rung true for me, and now I got to see it in real life! It made so much sense to me to work directly on this energy that runs in and around the body to support our physical form.

Needless to say, people swarmed to the front of the room at the end of the class with many questions. I had a question, too, about my mother's health and how to find a local graduate from her school for myself, but I knew I would probably never make it through the crowd to have my questions answered. I prayed for guidance, asking that if I was meant to have my questions answered, that I would somehow cross her path as I left. My attention then turned to gathering our things and making our way out of the room, not thinking any more about my questions.

I remember going down an empty hallway to get around the crowd with my wheelchair and with my mother who was hobbling along behind me on crutches with a severely deteriorated hip. As I turned the corner, suddenly there she was! Dr. Brennan looked as surprised to see me as I was to see her. She was headed for a book signing and was, amazingly, all by herself. I grabbed the opportunity to ask my questions. She quickly scanned my mother's energy and recommended Rolfing before having any hip surgery. She also told me how to get a list of graduates in my area. I was grateful for the gift of crossing her path. I had been recommending Rolfing to my mother for several months but she had been hesitant to go. After our encouraging meeting with Dr. Brennan in the hallway, my mother did make a move to receive several Rolfing sessions with Jan which clearly reduced her pain and suffering before surgery. As for me, it would take another year before I made my move to contact a BBSH (Barbara Brennan School of Healing) graduate for help. Little did I know that I would find another phenomenal woman who would not only help me move through multiple health issues, but also accelerate my spiritual awakening and help me usher in a more peaceful, healthy way to live.

Chapter 14

To Think It Is Educational,
To Believe It Is Transformational

...but it was in this constricting darkness that my attention and direction were turned onto a path that would bring a much deeper spiritual awareness to my everyday life...

The school year following Barbara's workshop in San Francisco was a tougher one for me. It was not my work schedule, the kids, or the staff. They all continued to give me great joy as I worked with them. It was my body. It did not want to be ignored any longer.

In an attempt to alleviate some of the strain, I had decided to leave my school of eleven years to work at another school within the district where I had access to a majority of the classrooms from inside the building and without doors, a disabled person's dream! This was one of the few healthy decisions I had ever made for my body. A couple of respiratory infections, muscles too weak to allow me to cough effectively, and increased muscle sensitivity to cold had successfully gotten my attention. I needed to spend less time outside in cold, wet weather, crossing the playground to get to the office or to classrooms. Dressing warmly had never been an option since even the weight of sleeves affected my movement. I was still traveling around the district a couple of days a week as well, which was more than enough time out in the elements.

But changing schools had not been enough. Late that spring I started experiencing extreme weakness and muscle fatigue throughout my body. It was different from anything I had ever experienced before. I was suddenly aware of my body's energy level as a whole and its inability to "charge" itself. Each morning I would wake up without regaining any stamina. Any reserves of strength or energy were being depleted. It was quite scary to feel myself drain so steadily and with what seemed like no control of my own.

By using far too much sheer will, I made it to the end of the school year, but then I had some serious thinking to do. If something did not change quickly, I would have to make drastic lifestyle changes and I was not ready for that. I was very emotionally attached to my "family" at work and did not want to leave them. I also feared I could not survive financially with all of my physical needs and without the income. This time, however, I could not look the other way. It was as if my body had decided that it was now in charge and was through with being forced.

I finally pulled out the BBSH list of graduates that I had requested almost a year earlier. Although I had thought all year about seeing someone, I was afraid my body might react poorly to the energy work rather than improve, and I was not ready to take the risk. After all, hadn't things gone inexplicably wrong so many times before when I tried to get my body help? I firmly believed that my body didn't react like everyone else's, and I certainly didn't trust it. But I was now desperate, and with no other option in sight, I finally made a move. I figured I had nothing to lose. In fact, I knew if I did nothing, I was sure to lose. Nothing like desperation to cut through fear! On the surface things were looking rather bleak, but it was in this constricting darkness that my attention and direction were turned onto a path that would bring a much deeper spiritual awareness to my everyday life and a transformed expansion of life force to support me in all ways. It was, in reality, a blessing.

I went through the list and made my choice, a woman named Patricia whose office was in the nearby town of Los Gatos. By the time I landed in her office in August 1997, I was drained, still sliding downward physically, and completely open to trying anything. My apprehension about the energy work was gone and I was ready for something good. I had done some soul searching earlier that summer while visiting my parents' cabin at Lake Tahoe, rolling up the canyon along the road by the creek searching for some spiritual answers. I finally found a sense of hope, and all I can say is that it felt like working with Patricia was going to be "big" somehow. There was even a sense of excitement about putting some focus on helping myself and not just others this time. I was not sure what to expect, but I knew I was in the right place.

I *thought* I was going to Patricia for purely physical reasons, to have some type of healing of my muscles so I could extend my strength and work longer. The physical, though, was just one slice of the pie. In Patricia, I *did* get someone who brings me incredible relief from those constant physical problems that my disability brings and that no one else medically has been able to address well. That has been miraculous in and of itself. But what I have also gotten, that has unfolded over the past ten years, is a more solid connection to my natural Divine Self and the power that goes with it to consciously create better experiences relating to my health and life in general. And because of the many experiences I have daily that confirm the presence of the Divine engaging and creating life with me, I've come to truly know and more fully trust these daily interactions and the support born of Grace. This has been an invaluable gift, a gradual shift away from the belief that I am predominantly on my own to survive, with a body destined for serious, long-term suffering. To *think* it is educational, to *believe* it is transformational. I needed immediate intervention with my body that could give me options and provide consistent, positive outcomes. I also needed a massive softening of my heart, a healing emotionally for myself and about myself, that could lead to a healthier body and a kinder, more peaceful, lifestyle despite my weakness. I needed my strong will to be instilled with wisdom.

It's a good thing I did not know in the beginning that I'd have to address my emotions and beliefs so deeply, because I'm sure I would not have believed it, would have said I did not need it, and would not have taken Patricia seriously. And if Patricia had known in the beginning how severely impaired and complicated I was physically, she might have referred me to someone whose primary focus and skills related to physical healings rather than spiritual awakening. Thank goodness we both were so strongly guided and only shown enough information at the time to get us started so that we would not make judgments that would get in the way.

I could not have selected a better match than Patricia, though I had no way of knowing at the time how truly profound her work would be with me. In addition to her training as an energy practitioner, Patricia was a teacher, a shaman, and was well educated in body psychotherapy, early childhood development, and transpersonal psychology. Her intuitive blending of skills, so perfectly given to ease my body and expand my soul awareness, continually amazes me. I believe that if I had found someone who had only addressed my physical body and not all of these areas, I could not have responded so amazingly well and I would not be experiencing the health and deep sense of peace that I have about life today.

I still remember the first session. We talked for a while about why I had come as she listened and intuitively read my needs. "It's really clear," she said. "You need to surrender." I gasped inside and felt my will fly right up to meet her. I challenged her statement immediately, thinking I had a ways to go to educate this woman about living as a successful handi. "Surrender?" I said in disbelief. "That's not how my body works, or my life, either. I have to take charge and direct my body with my thoughts, not just *let* things happen!" I said it calmly, but felt myself firmly "planted" in these statements and not willing to budge. What was she thinking, anyway? I was just sure that if I did not control every facet of my body, and the myriad of things related to it, that things would go downhill, fast. All she needed to do was spend a little time in my body, I thought, and she'd get it. Patricia attempted to explain what spiritual surrender meant, an expansion into the divine goodness that gently and wisely carries all of life, but I was not even close to being ready to hear it. So much

106

for thinking I was open to anything! Patricia had been correct, of course, about letting go so that life could right itself in a good way, but it would be many years before I honestly felt this was true.

During the first year Patricia spent each session charging and clearing my energy field, especially the lower chakras (energy centers/vortexes in the body) that fed my physical form. Since I'd had a lifetime of practice in how to avoid feeling negative emotion, fearing its effect would weigh down my physical movement, there was plenty for her to clear, and for years to come. I was so strong-willed that I'd learned to shut off feeling so I could push past lower-energy emotion such as fear, to do what I needed to do. Or at least I thought I'd pushed passed it. That heavy, dense energy of fear, and other lower-energy emotions related to it, were alive and well in my field, impeding a healthy flow of energy through my body. I needed that energy freed up, and the energy it unknowingly took to keep it suppressed, to support my body.

I felt immediate results from Patricia's work. I drove to a local drugstore to buy a birthday card, and having had only one session, I noticed a little more movement in my right arm to reach the cards on the lower shelf. Needless to say, I was thrilled! I had never before regained movement once it was gone, so this was exhilarating. The continuous feel of draining energy soon stopped, as well. My stamina returned and my arms felt less weighted. These may sound like small improvements, but they significantly enhanced my daily functioning for things as simple as brushing my teeth, feeding myself, and moving through the day. It was not only a physical relief, but also an emotional relief. I had found someone to help me and was no longer alone in trying to keep my body afloat.

I had no thoughts at the time of curbing my activity level. In fact, I was so relieved with the improvements that doing things was even more pleasurable to my don't-know-when-to-stop personality. The strain was lifted, and I relaxed a little about life. I was not expecting this energy work to be a miracle cure, but rather something that could buy me a little more time in the world of movement. I continued using the energy that was being freed up by Patricia's work, and then some, tapping much of the strength I had each day for several years until I finally had to stop.

You may be wondering why anyone with reasonable intelligence would expend such tremendous amounts of energy daily knowing she had so little to begin with. It would be more reasonable, one would assume, to guard muscle strength and do less instead of more. That didn't make sense to me, however. I enjoyed directing and leading things myself, and had no trouble putting in the effort if it was something I really wanted. I was less interested in using my energy to amass material things, and highly interested in using my energy to experience life and to help others. I took good care of the things I did acquire, like my house, my van, and my chair, out of respect for what I'd been able to receive to support my life.

In addition to these general personality traits, I had many beliefs that were "set in stone" that created this kind of drive in me, and an iron will that made sure that what needed to happen, happened. Some of my beliefs were floating, undefined, in the periphery of my consciousness. Others were more conscious but not up for questioning because I believed that's just how life was, or so I thought.

Though I'd had better medical results in my thirties, I still had many beliefs about living with my disability that were not so Grace-filled. Among them were beliefs about needing to force my muscles, being uncomfortable with asking for help, aligning myself to my profession and ignoring my disability, and beliefs in limited finances and resources once I could no longer work. I felt predestined to experience increasing physical pain and suffering as I grew weaker, especially related to muscle and joint pain and complications with breathing and swallowing. I believed suffering was inevitable and long-term, with no way out except to slow down the process.

In my mind, slowing down my decline meant pushing harder to keep it at bay, and finding metaphysical avenues for temporary relief. I was locked on to work as my life jacket, holding on to joyful purpose, to keep me afloat above the realm of dealing only with my body. The thought crossed my mind that I was to use every ounce of strength while working, and then one day simply drop in my tracks or maybe just mysteriously dissolve. These were not rational thoughts, but they felt very real. I was willing to use all my strength for what I loved, and once I could not work, I would deal with a dismal body I did not love. I was resigned to having to endure this forthcoming dark phase of my life, but found myself repeatedly attempting to ease or delay it.

As heavy as this may sound, I was not steeped in depression. Thank God my dominant beliefs and emotions were based in a love and joy of life. They are such a powerful force. The harder things got, the more practiced I became at staying mentally present. This allowed me to stay connected to the good of the moment and gave me maximum use of what I had mentally and physically for the task at hand. Giving to others and learning to stay present are what gave me the tremendous amounts of energy to do so much for so long, and they are what also kept me searching for the Grace that deepened my soul awareness. Fortunately, I was fueled by this energy daily. I enjoyed doing things with my dog, my family, and my friends. I enjoyed the outdoors, especially the mountains. I enjoyed the ability to be independent. I enjoyed supporting the students, staffs, and community at work and I felt loved and appreciated by them. I was highly motivated to continue doing and enjoying it all.

At the beginning of the second year of working together, Patricia began asking questions about how I felt regarding situations or events reflecting struggles with my weakness, fears of suffering, and the level of effort to do the basics of life. I honestly thought that I was fine, that it was just something I had to do, except for that inexplicable, massive wall of resistance that immediately rose up every time she tried to take my attention there. I did not know what that force of resistance was, but I would instantly shut down, stop talking, and feel myself retreat. It was the strangest, visceral reaction and so unlike my normally outgoing, verbal self. There was clearly no crossing that barrier through talking. Regardless of how she approached the topic, I felt myself shut down and retreat, adamant that I was not going there. And if I was not going "there," I certainly was not comfortable letting anyone else go there, either. I wasn't even sure what "there" was, but it felt very dark and that it needed to be guarded at all costs.

It took me years to accurately identify these emotions. They would well up from seemingly nowhere, heavy and dark, and I would have to sit with them after the session until I understood them. They seemed foreign, yet familiar. Even though I was extremely uncomfortable feeling vulnerable and delving into the shadows, I would have been more uncomfortable looking the other way while knowing something was there that I did not like and that took such charge of my reactions. My motivation to prolong my strength was also still high, so I pressed on. There was no turning back.

I think my resistance was especially strong because I knew Patricia was intuitively reading me like a book when it came to the emotions in my energy field even if I did not know them yet. I was a master at acknowledging positive emotions, which was unquestionably beneficial in dealing with life, but not to the extent that it completely denied all other emotions. Denying them felt like a basic survival tool, but I could no longer afford to hold that energy in my field and be weighted down by it. The toll was too high on my fragile body. The purpose it had served in the past was no longer serving me. My insistence on being happy needed to be the dominant emotion for me to acknowledge and maintain, but not the only emotion that I must learn to acknowledge. I would have to feel those unpleasant emotions for them to be energetically released and to usher in a better level of energy to run my body.

For the next several months, the sessions began the same way. Patricia would relax and get comfortable in her chair, sometimes unfocusing her eyes slightly as she went into her mode of reading my field and receiving guidance, and gently ask me what I was feeling... right now. My wall of resistance was always up by that point and in full control regardless how much I had promised myself I would not resist. It felt like a powerfully charged emotional reflex that defied logic and caused my eye contact to drop, my lips to close, and my jaw to lock shut. My mood would often shift to a general sense of anxiety and sadness, but that fiercely strong resistance of mine held me outwardly still and stoic. After some time of verbal impasse, Patricia would begin working on my field energetically to help loosen and clear the dark emotional energy and past traumas that were being stirred but that I could not begin releasing on my own.

I continued seeing Patricia every other week and sometimes more, hoping I could just make myself start talking while in her office when those heavy emotions floated up. That was so my style, to use force to make it happen. It was baffling to me that I excelled at being the communication specialist at work, but clearly not here. I became totally incapable of communicating as soon as I started to feel any emotional pain. Trying to force myself just seemed to make the resistance stronger. I soon realized I was there to heal emotionally from the inside out in addition to helping my body, and not by forcing with my will. I needed that dense energy to be dissolved slowly and pieces "loosened" so I could process them psychologically and release them. I don't believe a traditional counseling approach could have broken through my resistance.

I felt heavy-hearted throughout these months of attempting to engage with emotion, something I had never experienced before and most certainly not for any length of time. I was used to feeling fear and ignoring it, but feeling a sense of sadness was new for me. Going to work helped shift my attention away from myself for a welcomed breather. I was very private about what I was experiencing, so I did not share it with others and I'm sure no one even knew anything was "wrong." I trusted Patricia and the wisdom of the divine energy that brought us together. I knew the process had purpose for moving me toward good, even if it didn't feel good at the time.

After about seven months, I had a major release of resistance. I would like to say that the wall just vaporized one day or that I was successful in forcing through it myself, but that was not the case. Patricia, in her guided wisdom, announced that she could not make me talk or cry or anything else and she wasn't going to do a standoff (with my ego) any more. I wasn't sure if it meant we could not work together, but I didn't want to find out. I did not want to work on myself or deal with my body alone anymore, yet I knew she was right. Something had to change. By the time I got home I noticed the force of resistance had dropped, like letting go of a tug-of-war rope, but I honestly did not know if I would go back to silently pulling away again the next time we met since it seemed so automatic and beyond my control.

I had the need to email Patricia that evening after the session to explain what I thought might be going on with me. It took quite a while to formulate because I wasn't sure myself exactly what emotions I was feeling or why I resisted it all. It was a relief to find a way to communicate and I was able to explain some things in reflection that I had never been able to verbalize in the moment. And so began our "the session after..." emails for the next several years. Writing gave me an avenue for connecting more directly with my own divine guidance for introspection, self-analysis, and insight that I could share with another without meeting such internal resistance. The more often I wrote, the better I became at identifying feelings and thoughts that floated to the surface during our sessions, and identifying the beliefs that were enmeshed in them.

Defining my thoughts and sets of beliefs and observing how they created my experiences helped reinforce that they were indeed solidly present, which then gave me repeated opportunities to keep the thoughts and beliefs I liked and the choice to change what I did not like. The way I viewed the world was up for questioning in a big way, fueled by a need to avoid suffering and an emerging belief that a more peaceful body was possible. Patricia always sent a brief response to my emails, often just a line or two, but that was enough.

I was gaining some understanding, and I felt heard and supported. She gave me the freedom to delve into myself at my own rate and in my own way without judging how it was done, the perfect solution for a strong-willed person like me.

Now my learning significantly accelerated and my insights deepened with more wisdom. I became better at interrelating the events in my life as they wove a reflection of my way of thinking and feeling. Slight shifts in feeling/thinking/experiencing resulted in the unfoldment of long lasting changes regarding how I viewed myself and the world. I was greatly interested in understanding as best I could how my experiences fit into the big picture of moving me towards Good, especially when the experiences were far from pleasant. This took a vast amount of personal work and was not for the faint of heart! My emotional body is inextricably linked to my physical body, so there were times as I dove into old emotion and trauma (from this life and previous embodiments) that I truly felt my body was preparing to shut down and die, a pull towards death itself. These instances turned out to be ego deaths rather than physical deaths, a releasing of strong sets of beliefs that no longer served me and that needed to give way for a new way of being. I now had a new appreciation for the saying, "Old habits (of thinking) die hard!"

Clearing and charging my energy field actively and systematically stirred the dense energy of those not-so-Grace-filled thoughts. Some parts, I believe, were gently released from my field without my awareness while other parts needed to come to my awareness first, to be processed consciously before being released. This created space so that new beliefs more aligned with Divine truth could arise and take hold. Physical improvements, like extending my stamina and strength, then arose from that higher energetic level. Patricia's work and guidance moved me through this process more quickly and deeply than I could have ever done through verbal dialog alone— that is, if I had ever begun talking on my own!

As her work so demonstrably opened options and possibilities for my body with consistently positive results, it also opened my sight to options and possibilities relating to other areas of my life including getting a few of my needs better met. I found myself finally willing to ask for things at work to lessen my physical effort, such as a speakerphone, a laptop for traveling between schools, and eventually a part-time aide to help with the physical part of the job. The district, I found, was more than willing to support me. It was my own resistance to asking for help that had been in the way.

I began supporting my body in other ways as well, and as soon as I made the decision to do so, I found exactly what I needed. I went to a nutritionist and discovered I had hypoglycemia, which finally explained the sudden drops in energy and strength that I was experiencing. Adjusting my protein intake during the day to maintain blood sugar levels helped immensely. Since that was so successful, we even tried adding specific amino acids in the form of a specialized protein drink to rebuild the many amino acids that were completely depleted in my system. Thank goodness I started with a minimal dose, however, because the amino acids quickly became toxic to a body that had forgotten how to use them. About the same time I was also guided to a holistic clinic and began receiving regular B12 shots and other supportive supplements for my immune system. My body was incredibly responsive to the shots. I would feel a flush of well-being as soon as the dose entered my body, like the cells themselves were rejoicing from the nourishment, and I felt more charged. This proved helpful for several years. My willingness to begin giving my body more support was directly related to the softening of my beliefs regarding how I viewed myself and the world.

My gratitude for Patricia's work, and her friendship, is immeasurable. Twice a month for the past ten years, she has rolled up her metaphysical sleeves to relieve a seemingly endless array of health issues related to a lifetime of disability. I often say that if it hadn't been for her work, I would have slowly been crushed by the number of serious, chronic physical complications that I've experienced despite the strength of my own will to change or exist with them. My energy to turn inward would have been grossly hampered without relief from it, and the depth of my spiritual awakening would have not nearly been so great. Her work allowed my physical challenges to become increasingly manageable and often miraculously relievable. It also has given me time to "grow-up" spiritually so I could help support my own body with a stronger divine flow of energy. So with this relief and support, these challenges became the catalysts they were meant to be to take me repeatedly to my mental, emotional, physical, and spiritual edge for growth without taking me over the edge.

Chapter 15

Body Blowouts and a Heart Flung Open

I keep my thoughts directed to the task at hand to give me the power,
inch by inch, to complete the task.

All the grounding, clearing, and emotional work with Patricia had an unexpected benefit beyond my physical and emotional health. Occasionally when I would get ideas for myself or someone else, I started noticing a mild tingling response running up my legs, like a chill of sorts, but not from cold. After experiencing it numerous times, I realized that it was not random and was not like any other physical feeling with which I was familiar. It always seemed to come out of the blue to catch my attention about a thought I had just had, the words I had just spoken, or something I had just heard. It felt alive and communicative, like my body was feeling the vibration of someone excitedly emanating, "Yes! Good, that's it!" I was having my first spontaneous, perceptible interaction with Divine guidance that did not take a crisis to receive, the first of several ways of engaging with *It* that developed over the next several years.

Learning to feel more emotions while pursuing spiritual knowledge was the key to opening my ability to feel this tangible, interactive "conversation" with the Divine for guidance in everyday life. How odd, I thought. I'd practiced a lifetime of not feeling and tuning out my body because it so often had been a painful place to be, but I had actually needed the opposite. My body, to my surprise, was in tune to feeling guidance if I just brought my awareness to it enough to listen.

I did not find these experiences startling, just curious and somehow familiar. In fact, none of my experiences with Divine energy

117

have ever been scary regardless of how "out of the box" they have been. They have always felt strongly good and complete regardless of what I perceived at the time with my physical senses.

I had believed that we were given guardian angels and spirit guides to help us on our earthly journey (I've often joked that I must have been given an entire committee to help), but I never expected to actively engage with any. For me, it has been a consistently strong, wise, loving source of Grace, regardless of whether I mentally engage with it using semantic labels such as angels, guides, elemental or celestial energies, or God. It is my human need to verbally define it, though it goes beyond words. In actuality, it cannot be defined but only experienced. It's the feeling in the presence of *It,* a taste of our own true nature that is unmistakable, reassuringly familiar, and unwaveringly true. It is my experience that this Divine Presence is only divided into labels to help my fragmented mind grab onto a concept of wholeness and point me in Its direction.

Once I became aware of this tingling sensation of intuition, or energy rush as I called it, it took me quite some time to take the information seriously or trust its accuracy. Until I had enough concrete experiences in life to demonstrate that the information I received this way was *always right,* my logical mind prevailed and I continued to choose logic over intuition to make my decisions.

One experience that helped me trust my intuition related to finding attendant care. I had put my ad in the paper, set my intention, and asked for guidance. I did not want to feel such stress over finding the right person for the right hours yet again, so I attempted to relax into the process and trust that my needs would be met without struggling. After talking to one of the applicants by phone a couple of weeks later, I felt that familiar energetic rush I knew meant, "Yes!" I was surprised at its interjection, and mentally replied, "She's the one? Are you sure?" I was answered by another energy rush, an affirmative response as definitive as the first. Nevertheless, I was reluctant to trust the guidance I had asked for because the person was not outwardly someone I would have chosen. I did include her in a follow-up interview because of the guidance and liked her as a person, but my beliefs about whom I should chose from past experience overrode my willingness to trust guidance. My guidance said, "yes" but my brain said "no," so I chose someone else.

The woman I chose, who seemed outwardly perfect, did not work out, however. She had repeated, unexpected problems arise almost immediately that kept her from coming consistently even though I believe she had good intentions about working with me. Something inexplicable was happening that kept getting in the way. By the end of two months, it was clear that I needed to find someone else and that I should have trusted my guidance instead of my logic. I called back the first woman, and to my relief she was still available to help. She turned out to be reliable, kind, and a great assistant who worked with me for the next three years. From that point on, I put more trust in those intuitive "Yes's" when they were spontaneously offered as my primary adviser for making decisions.

Guidance and insight began appearing in other ways as well. I would suddenly have clarity about something that did not come from my usual train of thought. In fact, I knew it was guidance precisely because it did not follow a sequence of thoughts, but rather entered as a complete thought of its own which contained wholeness, purpose, and meaning. It helped put pieces together into "the big picture," resonated as true, and felt peaceful.

Similar guidance also began appearing at night with insights of even greater magnitude. There were several years that I found myself awake at 1:00 a.m. or 2:00 a.m., listening to someone from my dreamtime as I was waking. The information brought me insights about myself and often tied together events that had seemed random during my waking-time, giving them meaning and purpose for my spiritual unfoldment. This "download" of information was more readily understood in an expanded state of being as I came out of sleep, where the intricate interrelatedness of life is more obvious.

Sometimes I could retain all the information for verbal replay in my head, and sometimes it was too great to define with words alone and its deep meaning would fade back into my subconscious.

I also began acknowledging some vivid dreams that either felt powerful and/or followed a repeated theme related to my physical life. Some dreams appeared to be healings, like the one I had several times where I visited the home of a married couple. Their home and backyard felt familiar, and by the end of the dream one or both of them had given me a healing of some sort. Other dreams were unmistakably symbolic regarding my approach to life with a will that seemed unstoppable. In all cases the dreams felt significant and well developed, and their detail did not fade with time.

I am alone on a dry, dirt trail that follows the hillside to my left and a ravine to my right. It is summer. The land is desolate, seemingly devoid of plant and animal life. My entire focus is upon getting to the small town I see in the distance about five miles away at the end of the ravine. I am seated in a manual wheelchair, my weak hands grasping the wheels to push with all my strength only to move the chair a few inches at a time. I do not see this as an impossible task. I am familiar with the effort it takes to do things. I am determined to do it myself. I keep my thoughts directed to the task at hand to give me the power, inch by inch, to complete the task.

The dream's message was clear to me about the way I still approached life. My will was out of control. I was determined to do things myself, utilizing tremendous intent and focus, regardless of the level of effort or how ridiculous the task had become for my body. I still believed in forcing, if that's what it took, to get things done in the day. And forcing seemed to be necessary for more and more parts of my day.

Someone once commented to me that they thought the benefit of having such a significant physical impairment was that it must have taught me to have healthier boundaries than the average person about not over-doing. I was so surprised by her statement that I laughed out loud! I told her that the opposite had been true. My boundaries were grossly distorted by having always pushed against my physical limits that I was the *worst* example of a person with healthy boundaries. I admitted that I often had to crash figuratively and skid eighty feet or so, and after the third or fourth crash, then maybe I'd contemplate a change.

I was well aware of this behavior by now, but was not very good at correcting it. I knew I was making gains in softening my beliefs about how I approached life with this body of mine, but my body still felt like such a hindrance. I understood *cognitively* what Patricia was telling me about things like listening to my body, stopping before I was wiped out, being willing to ask for help, and trusting that I had other options, but I couldn't always *apply* it. I could say it, knew I needed to do it, but often didn't change because it just didn't feel right yet. There was resistance to feeling and believing that I did not need to drive my body that often seemed to stop me. Luckily, Patricia's work, in conjunction with the continued events of my life, slowly broke loose some of my most rigid thoughts about balancing how I treat my body with what I do in life.

As the gap widened between my physical strength and my ability to maintain my independent, working lifestyle, I began having more regular health problems, or "body blowouts" as I called them, from the increasing strain of conducting the day. Although I was trying to be more aware of my body's messages, I usually didn't pick up on them until after they were strong enough to create a physical issue. I still had a huge disconnect between my mind and my ability to read my body, even with the knowledge and insights I was gaining about doing life differently. I did not see the direct connection between these blowouts and my overdrive. I thought they were simply part of life with a disability. I was so good at not looking at my body's frailty for fear it might stop me that I had completely lost the ability to read its exhaustion levels.

Over the next few years I seemed to have less time feeling good and more time dealing with health issues, general strength, and stamina. This included bouts of serious dehydration, diverticulitis, shingles, and headaches. I became more susceptible to colds, something that had rarely been a problem in the past. Nerve, joint, and muscle pain would have become chronic, but was highly responsive to Patricia's work. In fact, as each health problem arose, Patricia helped me move through them with considerably less strain, including so many rounds of passing kidney stones that I can't even count. Her tenacity for clearing and charging my energy field revived me over and over again.

The harder things got for me physically, the more I leaned into my dog, Zinkle, for help. She was almost eleven by now, but as eager to work as ever. We worked intricately throughout the day, a testimony to the benefits of a strong soul connection and true teamwork. There wasn't much I did physically that did not involve her.

So when Zinkle collapsed one fall morning and did not have the energy to get up, my heart fell. I rushed her to the vet, who saw the gravity of her condition and sent us to an emergency clinic that was open on the weekend. By the time we arrived at the emergency clinic, she had already lost a third of her blood from a ruptured growth on her spleen. She had dutifully walked in even though she was in shock, and while she was getting some hydration and medication intravenously, I agreed to surgery on the small chance that the tumor was not cancerous. The vet, who was teary-eyed with me, made it clear that if the growth were malignant, she would call me but not wake Zinkle out of surgery.

Another vet was to be called in for the procedure. I would not be able to wait with Zinkle in the room with all the other injured animals, they said, but I could visit with her before I left. As my chair began to move with a click of the motors, I heard a vet tech say from the other room, "Hey! Where are you going?" That familiar click to Zinkle meant we were on our way, and she was ready to jump off the table, I.V. tubing and all, to follow my chair as she had done so automatically over the past eight and a half years.

I entered the room to find her quite alert. She was lying down but sitting up on her elbows on the exam table. As I rolled up alongside the table, Zinkle stretched her right front leg gently off the side to rest it in my lap so that I could touch her. I did not want to cry or say goodbye for now. I desperately wanted somehow to hold open an energetic possibility for her to be well. Although I was full of grief with the probability of losing her, Zinkle did not seem worried at all about her situation. She was clearly more concerned about the crying dog in a nearby kennel, who had just awakened from surgery. I stayed for a few minutes, too choked up to say much of anything except to tell to her briefly what was going to happen and that I would be back. They placed her in a kennel, and when I left I glanced up to see her expectant face looking at me as they closed the kennel door.

A few hours later I got the call that the tumor was malignant, and that they were stopping surgery to put her to sleep. I hung up and felt numb. Then a profound sense of loss and grief flooded my heart. I was losing her. I had wanted to be with her as she left so she would not feel alone, but that was a physical impossibility. What was I to do? Zinkle had always been there for me, and now it was my turn. So I closed my eyes and sat quietly to connect to her energetic presence, feeling mine blend into hers as she left. I thanked her for all she had done for me, and for the first time since I was young, a few tears surfaced to roll down my cheeks. We were so close that I knew she would feel me.

What a loss for me. I don't remember the rest of that day, but I do remember that my roommate, Mariana, had a great idea to light a candle outside that night in tribute to Zinkle. It was a crisp, quiet fall evening. Our hearts were heavy as she set the dish with the candle on the patio table, lit it, and remarked, "This is for a great dog." We certainly didn't expect what happened next. Our solemn mood was suddenly uplifted with an unmistakable chorus of dogs barking all around the neighborhood! At first it started with only a few, but it quickly escalated until there were so many barking dogs that it made us laugh. We rarely heard any dogs barking, so this was quite unusual. We could only surmise that Zinkle's exuberant presence had come rushing in when we called, just as she had always done while in physical form. As incredible as it may sound, there was no mistaking Zinkle's presence and how it had been felt by the dogs around the entire block. She certainly had gotten their attention and, in the process, our attention, too. It was comforting to know that she was still present in such a strong, happy way. This was the first of many experiences to remind me that the physical and non-physical worlds are not separate, and that our heart connection would remain forever strong.

My students were such a help in working through Zinkle's death. Some adults seemed hesitant to look at me, afraid to bring the subject up because it was so painful, but not the kids. "Are you sad, Miss Laraway?" they'd ask, as they looked me straight in the eye. They were genuinely concerned, open with their own feelings about missing her, and wanting to know what I would do without her. Since I worked with many children in groups all day long, I had a chance to talk quite a bit about her, which was very healing. Children ask honest questions and want honest answers. It was the perfect way to keep me honestly talking to them about emotion, good memories, and loss. I think this was the first time I had ever talked to anyone in person about something painful. It was one of several healing gifts I was to receive from Zinkle's passing.

The students and staff wanted to do something to commemorate Zinkle's life. My principal decided to have a "Penny Drive" so that all students could participate in making a donation to CCI. The students brought in and rolled $500 worth of pennies, and with donations from the staff and from around the district, a total of $1,500 was collected. The donations bought training items and toys for dogs in advanced training as well as two inscribed pavers with

Zinkle's name and a message, one from the students and one from district staff, placed in the courtyard at CCI.

Zinkle's inimitable presence graced my day twice more within the next several weeks. The first occurred when my friend, Maria, and I had stopped in at the emergency vet clinic to get Zinkle's ashes. As the receptionist approached the counter with the box of ashes, the box mysteriously jumped from her hands and flipped onto the counter! The poor receptionist paused in disbelief, since she had held the box with both hands from the bottom and there was no obvious explanation for what had just happened. She apologized and then examined the box carefully for damage, afraid I'm sure that I might be upset. I was far from upset. It was all I could do to hold back my laughter. Those were Zinkle's ashes, all right! Her personality had remained, I thought, even in ash form. I immediately sensed her presence and the words, "Where have you been?" came to mind. As we left, I told Maria to hold on tight to that box as we laughed and chatted all the way to the van about what had happened. Any surge of grief marked by the finality of holding her ashes was changed to joy by that experience. I was glad to have had such a physical response to reuniting with my dog.

Zinkle's presence appeared again a few weeks later on a Saturday afternoon as I was slowly trying to complete some paperwork at the dining room table. To say that I had not been well since her death would be an understatement. I was suffering from the deepest fatigue I had ever felt that clouded my thinking, affected my memory, and gave me a general feeling of having the flu. The instability of not having my dog had been compounded almost immediately by also losing my morning attendant without notice. I had been struggling to find ways to get up in the morning for the past several weeks until I found someone more permanent to replace her. Needless to say, life was hard.

My cousin and brother had invited me to go to the mall that Saturday in November, but I was too drained and needed to use the little energy I had to get some basic things done at home. My cousin loved candles, so during their outing she bought me one, brought it by, and lit it at my table before they left. I had never been one for lighting candles, for safety reasons, since I am so limited physically, but for some reason I decided it was fine. I didn't think any more about the candle and went back to my paperwork, trying to focus on the task despite the fog in my head and my body's fatigue.

Not long after it was lit, something strange happened. Out of the corner of my eye I saw the flame bounce briefly in an animated way and trail smoke off its tip. It did not truly hold my attention until the third time, when it bounced so strongly and trailed so much smoke that I could not miss it. This was no ordinary candle flame movement. "Zinkle, is that you?" I asked incredulously. The flame bounced excitedly and trailed more wisps of smoke. I looked around the room. There was nothing that would have moved the air to create such an effect. Sometimes it swayed back and forth like her beautiful golden tail, sometimes it bounced as if to say "yes," and other times the flame stood perfectly still until I hit a "yes" question. There was no doubt for me that my dog's soul was present and trying to get my attention. The experience was not scary, but calming, and very real. I felt like I had a full conversation with her that day, as a wise expanded soul now out of her canine wraps. Her presence continued to visit me often through this medium for several years, and always put a smile on my face.

Zinkle's death broke my heart. Any vestige of resistance to feeling genuine emotion was literally blasted apart. I had become quite dependent upon her physical and emotional support as I pushed through my day, and now she was gone and it felt like part of me was gone, too. But behind that pain and loss laid two hidden blessings, the silver lining in the proverbial black cloud. First, I had a marked increase in intuition that seemed to come through my heart. If the heart is said to be the doorway to the divine, I'd had my doorway suddenly flung open. And the more I asked for and received guidance through this opening, the more I felt supported by life. This deeper interaction between the Universe and me came in part, I believe, because I was willing to keep my heart open for Good and not play victim. I gained greater trust in its wisdom for guiding me towards Good, even through devastation.

The second blessing was equally as important. Up to that point I had been unable to shed a tear while working with Patricia or on my own regardless of how strong an emotion I felt. The more I needed to cry, the stronger my resistance would become not to cry, and this seemed to be beyond my control. It took me years to realize that crying actually had felt shameful and unsafe for some reason. My only explanation for having this kind of abnormal reaction for such a basic human response was that I must have practiced it as a survival strategy over many lifetimes. To avoid the resistance, Patricia had taught me to feel emotional pain and release its energy through exhalation, which I still use today. With Patricia's direct work and by using this technique, my resistance to feeling emotional pain had been getting whittled away, but I had a long way to go. I needed something big to break through it if I were to make real progress, and nothing could have touched my heart more deeply than the death of my canine partner. Although crying remains difficult, it has become more spontaneously natural and I am more comfortable in letting it be. I am grateful to Zinkle for being the one to begin that healing for me.

Patricia suggested a few months later that I hold a ceremony outside to get some closure energetically and emotionally since I was having trouble letting Zinkle go, and feeling drained. I held a simple ceremony in gratitude to her with my parents, roommate, and a friend. We buried the ashes from her picture, some dog treats, and her favorite food, corn on the cob. In addition to this, I wrote her a final goodbye letter as I had done with Isaac. It was a painful time for me.

It's time to say goodbye, Zinkle

It's been three months since you've left
and I've had a hard time letting you go.
The loss is only matched by how much I loved you.

You looked so happy on that exam table
wagging your tail as I entered,
licking my face, and draping your front leg over my arm
and into my lap to be with me.
You were content with life just as it was.

They said I couldn't stay. They had to call in a surgeon.
I didn't want to leave you.
So when they called to say you had cancer
and would not be awakened from surgery, I cried.
I wasn't ready to say goodbye.
So how do I say goodbye to the half that helped me
function as a whole?

I miss your excitement about everything,
your love of work and play,
your profound perceptions and intelligence,
your desire and ability to communicate,
and your openness to become one with me.

You were a happy dog that subtly took over more and more
as I subtly have grown weaker and weaker.
I miss your expectant face when I come into a room,
the warmth of your body on my bed at night,
your nose flipping my arm on your back to be petted,
your head on my foot at work.

No more treks up the canyon to play in the creek,
no sniffing on the trails at your favorite oak park,
no chasing the ball that rolled off my lap
because I could not throw it.
You didn't care that the ball didn't go far, you made it a game
and ran with it because everything was fun for you.

128

Now the briefcase you carried for me sits on the shelf,
everything gets shoved in a backpack for work,
and all the things I drop stay on the floor, all now out of reach.

I have to work at opening my own doors
and turning on my own lights
and I am so disabled without you.

I woke up at night last week, feeling how strongly united I still felt
even though you're not here, and not knowing how to let go.
How do I say goodbye to my partner of so many years?

I asked you to teach me how to let go,
how to say goodbye, because I didn't know how to do it.
You didn't make me wait long,
and as your response drifted in, I knew it was you.

"Release!" you said, something so perfectly simple
yet all encompassing, a command you knew well.

So release, Zinkle, it's time to go play with Isaac.
I now know why his name came up several times
the week before you died. I think he was waiting for you.
You had big shoes to fill and you did it well
with your own energetic style.

Thank you for coming and helping me.

Chapter 16

Hold Steadfast and Move

Sometimes we believe in divine intervention intellectually, but to observe its manifestation unfold before us is truly amazing.
It was a match made in heaven...

It became evident after Zinkle's death that the persistent, extreme exhaustion I'd been feeling was stemming from something more than emotional loss. It was different from any weakness or physical fatigue with which I was familiar. I felt drained and had a deep sense of mental exhaustion that made my thinking cloudy. I had difficulty focusing and remembering, organizing, or being spontaneously articulate, all of which had previously been effortless. It was often accompanied by dull headaches and a general sense of not being well. I became aware of my body's flow of energy, which literally felt as though I were coughing and sputtering like an old truck on a cold morning. Everything took much more effort and I felt bogged down, symptoms I had previously felt only briefly and to a lesser degree. I made it through each day doing only what had to get done at work and at home.

After about two months, I was desperate for some relief. I went to the doctor for blood work, which showed that I was anemic, and that my thyroid activity was somewhat deficient, both of which could cause fatigue. I was glad that something had been identified and that it was correctable with supplemental iron and thyroid medication. However, after many months I was not feeling better even though my blood work had improved. If it had not been for another speech pathologist who happened to be supervising a student placed in my program for field experience, I may not have discovered the cause of the problem for some time. The supervisor also had polio as a youngster, although her resulting disability was much milder than mine, predominantly affecting one leg. She, too, had been experiencing excessive fatigue and decreased muscle strength to the point that it was significantly affecting her daily functioning. And like me, she also could no longer push through her symptoms to move through the day by sheer willpower.

I was surprised that we were experiencing some of the same symptoms, especially the debilitating fatigue, since she was so much stronger than I. It was the perfect time for her to cross my path, and clearly a gift of Grace to bring me some much needed insight once again. After talking to her and reading the articles she had given me on Post-Polio Syndrome (PPS), I realized that many of the challenges I was having with my body that I thought were unrelated, were not, and that my struggles were not because I was not trying hard enough. They were part of a group of symptoms being reported by a large number of post-polio survivors that frequently appear several decades after the initial illness. What also caught my attention, and appropriate to my situation, was that an acceleration of symptoms and their severity can occur after a physical or emotional trauma. The loss of my dog, I now realized, had helped to trigger severe chronic fatigue and rapid muscle decline.

The most effective intervention for alleviating many of the PPS symptoms is to lessen the strain on the body, slow down, and take frequent rests. This sounds like a relatively easy solution. However, the changes I'd already made had not been sufficient to improve my health, and I could not see how to do life any differently and still have the financial resources to remain living at home. In addition, since I'd predominantly used my driven personality to run my life, it was hard to let go and trust that something better could emerge. I was not ready yet to surrender completely to the stream that carries life.

I continued through the school year with minimal strength and repeated health issues stemming from the strain. I miraculously had just enough energy and strength to do the day, but I felt systemically ill and was so drained that nothing seemed to bring me joy. It felt as though life had slowly gone from living color to black and white. I was in survival mode. By spring I felt I had no choice but to decrease my time at work to 70%. My resistance to this change had been high, but immediately lessened once I'd made my decision, and the energy I was using to hold that resistance was now free to create something new. What had felt like a difficult, scary decision, once it was made, brought me a sense of relief and a slight shift towards well-being. I have learned that looking back only lessens my ability to manifest my needs, and is as effective as trying to reverse current on a charged electrical line. Therefore, I shifted my focus from the past to following through with the present changes and used my will to minimize any of my own conflicting thoughts. This is where I've found my strong will to be of greatest benefit in my own spiritual awakening: once I make a decision, I hold steadfast and move with it without looking back so that doubt cannot weaken its force. I was ready for some relief and improved health, something I was finally willing to give myself, and I now had to trust that things would work out financially.

This was a good step for me, reflecting a growing willingness to feed some energy and care back into myself rather than viewing my body as a lost cause and driving it to complete depletion. It was another softening of how I treated myself and a strengthening of my trust in divine order and support to get my needs met, a shift that breathed a bit of life back into me. I needed to use my strong will for a new job: to hold a larger space for Grace to enter, instead of using my will to force life.

It would be so much easier if the stronger the need, the easier it was to trust life and calmly relax into receiving Grace. However, my fear was so strong that I had to use strong will and discipline to minimize negative thoughts and to apply the principles of Divine Law for things I really needed related to my disability, even though I'd had repeated experiences in its ability to bring forth tremendous good. I was realizing that doubt usually piggybacked on fear, and the higher my need, the stronger my fear of not getting those needs met. Illness and exhaustion added to the struggle. Nevertheless, each experience over the years had been building a more solid foundation for me to challenge and move through greater fears to arrive at the greater good that was waiting behind them. It was in these experiences that I became the most motivated to find relief, to question my perceptions of reality that defined what I thought was possible, to release some of my strong ego control, and to build a different kind of strength. Reducing my workload would give me practice in all of these areas and prepare me to handle even bigger challenges to come.

I was sure that having fewer days at work would make a significant impact on improving my health and offer me more years to work. There would be time each week without the usual body demands, something I had never given myself in my adult life, that would give me some recharging time. Other avenues of support were on the horizon as well. After five years of persistence, I had finally secured funding for the adaptive equipment on a new van that would be better tailored to my current ability levels. Although there was much to do physically to complete the strenuous driving evaluation and to get the vehicle fitted to my needs, the van was on its way and would be ready by fall. I was also scheduled for two weeks of team training at CCI in August to get another service dog. I was relieved that these major reinforcements were coming together to support me so I could lessen my expenditure of strength each day. I was also aware and concerned that the process of getting them would continue to tax my body's reserves.

Participating in the two-week training for another service dog was much harder this time because of my fatigue and weakness. It had been almost a year since Zinkle's death. I knew I did not have the strength now to both drive myself and participate in the training. Fortunately, I had purchased a used adapted minivan a few years earlier, one that I could be driven in, so this became the perfect solution. How relieved I was to be driven so I could use the energy I did have for training with a new dog! I maximized my stamina and strength during training by mentally staying as present as possible, affirming how I wanted the day to go, and keeping a balanced intake of food and water. Though the days were long, the CCI staff was as caring, energetic, and supportive as ever, so it was not difficult to enjoy the experience.

I was placed with an intelligent yellow lab named Plato whom the staff felt had great potential for meeting my needs. However, it was clear after graduating and being home for several weeks that our partnership was not developing. Despite all of his training and abilities and a tremendous amount of effort on my part to encourage and work with him, we were not connecting. Unlike my other dogs who loved this kind of interaction, it was obvious to me that he did not. It felt as though he somehow understood what was expected of him for the long term, that he did not want it, and that his well-developed consciousness knew it. He could complete the tasks, but it truly did not interest him. I do believe he felt the work he was doing in training was temporary and that he'd go home to play when it was done. I was amazed at his level of thinking and how clear he was about what he wanted in life. Many people reading this will not believe that dogs have the ability to perceive at these levels, but that has not been my experience. These dogs, with their multi-generational breeding history of strong human-animal bonding, communicate quite clearly and deeply if we know how to listen. Plato was not a bad dog, but this kind of calling was not in his heart nor could it be taught, yet it is essential for a happy, solid partnership. It is an innate quality of the soul that I used to think was only relevant to humans. My time with him changed my thinking.

I tried every technique I knew to motivate him with advice from the trainers but to no avail. His reluctance persisted; he began growling at unfamiliar noises and was generally uneasy. I had been asking my inner guidance all along if he was the right dog since our work had felt uphill from the beginning, and the answer was always a clear "yes." Because my guidance had always been right, I kept trying to make changes to my part of our interaction in order to make our connection work. All the while, however, I kept thinking this boy needed a boy, someone who could be more physical with him at play and for reward. He needed to work a little and play a lot.

My guidance was indeed correct, but it took me a while to understand just what our purpose together was all about. He was the right dog for me—not as a partner, but for spiritual growth. I needed to stop trying to make things work that were obviously not right, something I needed to do in other areas of my life as well. Plato was a good teacher. He was clear about what he wanted in life, and I needed to be also. So after six weeks of effort and much soul searching, I gave him back to CCI. It was difficult to admit that I couldn't make it work, but I knew that once I got over myself, it was the best decision for both of us. There was a great sense of relief that came with letting go. I desperately needed life to flow more easily and so did he.

The trainers were extremely supportive and about two months later I returned to CCI to be matched with a dog beyond my wildest dreams. Jeannie, a beautiful black lab/golden retriever cross, was nothing short of a miracle. From the first time we met, there was an instant bond and by the second day, I can honestly say that I felt like we'd been together forever. My stamina and strength by now were marginal, exhausted from the emotional and physical strain of the past thirteen months.

I needed our relationship to come together easily, and it did. Jeannie stepped in effortlessly, eager to join into my world, and immediately looked for her part in my movement. We had an instant intuitive connection which made training a breeze. Within four days we had skills together as though we'd been training the full two weeks, and we passed the practical test in the community without a hitch. We returned home and started work immediately. Jeannie blended into routines everywhere with grace and wisdom, far beyond her young age, and at levels that defied logical expectation. Her forty-five command repertoire remarkably expanded in less than two months to the sixty-five commands that Zinkle had learned, something unheard of even for a champion service dog. Jeannie possessed the best characteristics of my first two dogs: the calm, depth of soul and persistent focus of Isaac, and the work drive and interactive communication abilities of Zinkle. It was a dynamite combination. She was serious when she worked, silly when she played, and could bounce between work and play with ease. The assistance, joy, and stability she brought me were an incredible gift.

Experiencing our immediate, deep connection and the uncanny way Jeannie read my needs left no question in my mind that something wonderful was happening at a non-physical level to create such an outcome. Sometimes we believe in divine intervention intellectually, but to observe its manifestation unfold before us is truly amazing. It was a match made in heaven, given perfectly in response to my need and beyond my imagination, and without much effort on my part to direct its appearance. In fact, when I made the decision to release Plato, I knew I had to be comfortable with having no dog at all. I believe the personal decisions I made regarding Plato and my openness to the outcome created a pathway for the right dog to enter, though I did not know it at the time.

And in this divine exchange where all my needs were met, Plato's needs were met, too. He was released from the program and placed with a single mom and her son who was dealing with a reoccurrence of bone cancer. Plato had the perfect skills for accompanying the boy to hospital visits and being his buddy. I received a photo a couple of months later of Plato lying on the couch next to the boy, and both looked very happy. *My boy finally had his boy.* It was yet another experience to show me the importance of asking for guidance, staying as present as possible, and doing what feels right each step of the way so I could be led to the best outcome rather than trying to be the dominant force in creating it all. Experiences like this have continued to build my trust in the consistent support of Grace that enters even more strongly when I hold an open intention towards my greatest good and move along that well-beaten path through thought to connect and receive it.

Jeannie and I looking at all the minnows in Taylor Creek near South Shore, Lake Tahoe.

Chapter 17

Control Tower Down

*It was as if the universe was carrying me with enough
external movement to stay afloat until I could let go
and make an internal move towards health.*

I now had a more manageable workload, a well-matched vehicle, and service dog to lessen the load, but my body continued to spiral downward at a rapid rate. I had created magnificent support, but I was still resistant to the bigger personal changes needed for me to be well, so the support was not sufficient to keep up with the dramatic physical changes. The excessive fatigue was relentless; health problems were still occurring one after another, and what little muscle strength I had was disappearing fast. By now I had forgotten what it was like to feel good. Although I felt like I was running on vapors I kept going, set on extracting every ounce of strength toward maintaining the life that I knew even though I was miserable. I was so focused on straining to keep things the same that I could not even begin to dream of anything different.

I was struggling but not wanting to admit to myself that I could not control or force my body anymore. My thinking was so cloudy from fatigue and resistance that I miserably trudged along even though I knew I was not healthy or happy. I was locked into rigid thinking that allowed for no options except to become more drained. I believed it was just part of life with a disability. As I had seen the rate of my physical limitations increase over the previous couple of years, I found myself literally bargaining with Grace, the source that was so obviously sustaining me despite my own weighted thoughts, to keep me going a little longer. Once all possibility of maintaining my current work schedule was gone, then I promised my body it could lead even if that meant doing nothing. In fact, I assumed it meant doing nothing. Despite all the expansive thinking and successful outcomes I had experienced in other areas of my life, including some aspects of my body's health, my general set of beliefs about my body was still greatly based in lack and fear. The theme of unstoppable deterioration, dead-ends, and no visible options still held strong, yet my will pulled relentlessly against this. No wonder I was exhausted.

I was clearly being given spiritual free will, but my choices were driven by fear rather than wisdom. I was aligning to personal will rather than trusting divine will, and I felt boxed in, contracted, and miserable. Even in this misaligned state, however, I couldn't help but notice the strong current of divine energy that filled and moved me daily even though my muscles felt collapsed. I really was doing the impossible physically. I knew I wasn't functioning "on my own." What I was accomplishing daily, I couldn't do alone with my marginal strength. It was as if the universe was carrying me with enough external movement to stay afloat until I could let go and make an internal move towards health. Thank goodness that Grace is strong and patient. The heavens indeed had better plans, but I had to be the one to make the move in that direction.

A grand physical catastrophe could have forced a change, but luckily my well-worn path to divine guidance and support saved me. One spring morning that year I awoke "knowing" that my current situation could no longer be supported. The message was clear, simple, and felt solidly true. I knew there would be no more negotiating, and that if I ignored the message, greater suffering could not be helped because I was so out of balance.

I felt the seriousness of what I was being told. It did not feel punitive, just directly honest. Who knows what went on while I was asleep that night to have carried such a strong message forward. I can only imagine the amount of discussion that occurred between

140

my soul and those who guide me. I knew a decision had been made at an esoteric level and that I must act on it and not waver. I was surprised how calm and sure I felt, along with a glimmer of relief. The resistance of decades was suddenly lifted, and I knew I must retire. Staying was no longer an option. I had to trust that life would carry me.

I think it came as a total shock to everyone when I announced my retirement. I had maintained such a strong outer facade and managed well enough at work that no one knew how weak and ill I was. In fact, I was so steeped in trying to hold life together that even I did not know how bad my condition had become. Miraculously, my students were still flourishing even though I was not. The district was supportive and open to making changes if that would help me stay. However, I knew that nothing would be sufficient for my needs to be met short of stopping, and I had to have faith that my students and staffs would get their needs met, too, without me. I had no idea how I would get medical coverage, live on half my salary, or what would become of me. I knew I needed to step back and be led once again by the Grace of God. I could not direct this time. I needed so much more than I could even think of creating. I needed to have a much greater force for good completely create life for me.

All the practice in trusting life the year before had been a warm-up exercise in trusting divine law, asking for guidance and divine intervention, and letting go of the outcome. I now applied all of this on a much greater scale. The profound fatigue and long-time strain ultimately served to crack open my unhealthy, driven will. I now had to fully surrender and let go, something I had never done so deeply before. I was suddenly willing to allow life to unfold, too exhausted to argue with myself any longer, but also surprisingly hopeful that I could find peace of mind. Though the decisions were hard ones, I felt a great sense of calmness despite the magnitude of the tasks, a sure sign that I was aligning myself closer to divine will and to a good outcome. I was honestly willing to ask the universe to lead me, and I allowed myself to collapse. As fear would rise, I'd breathe it out slowly through my heart, ask for the thoughts to be replaced with divine truth and options, and "right myself" into a space of trusting that I would be okay no matter what happened. I had to be okay; I had no choice. That included accepting the thought of living in a residential facility if that would give me the consistent care I needed, and finding goodness there, too. Even that thought gave me relief.

I had no idea when I started school that year that it would be my last. However, I suspect that Grace had known. That fall I had a sudden, happy desire to schedule a cruise to Alaska for the following summer. It is extremely difficult for me to travel, so this was an unusual impulse. I rarely travel at all except to my parents' place at the lake for a visit in summer. I did cruise once to Alaska out of Vancouver in the early 90s with some friends, and had a spectacular time taking in the pristine, natural environment found in that region. I never thought I would be able to go again, though, because air travel was hard on my fragile body and on my equipment. I was already exhausted, so the idea of expending extra energy to organize and problem-solve all the details should have met resistance. However, it did not. In fact, it was exactly the opposite experience. I should have suspected that this idea was "Grace-driven" by the way the thoughts seemed to appear out of the blue, by the strong, joyous desire that arose when I thought about the possibility of it, and by the calm certainty that it would happen.

By leaving from San Francisco, and avoiding flying, the cruise was possible. All I had to do was roll out of the van and roll right onto the ship. That simplified things dramatically, caused no strain on my body, and made the idea of a trip possible. Five of my friends were willing to go, buy their own tickets, and help with my attendant care. Finding and paying for care is always a huge hurdle for me in traveling and was amazingly solved by some very good friends. This was a wonderful group to be with, as you can well imagine, and the cruise gave me an opportunity to experience something truly enjoyable during a time when life was tough. I had good food, fun friends, and wondrous scenery.

The trip landed perfectly at the end of my career, a heavenly bon voyage, and at a time when I was the most depleted and un-well. It was the consummate gift for my situation, and not one I would have ever planned if I had known I was not going to be working. Thank goodness none of these thoughts had been in the way during planning, because everything indeed worked out well, including the money. It was good to be away from home without the usual demands of the day and to be able to do as little or as much as I wanted. It was exceptionally timed for getting my driven mind to slow down and for allowing my body a much needed break. I spent most of my time relaxing on deck with hot tea, basking in the unusually warm weather, and thoroughly enjoying my friends, the scenery, and the chance to see marine animals. I felt soothed by the gentle rocking of the boat as I slept, spiritually drawn to the serenity of the land and quiet ocean inlets, and well cared for. I was so ready to be still.

A few weeks later, I had a flash of life beyond the one I had known. I found myself wondering what it would be like to roll along on a walk with Jeannie, feeling relaxed and at peace. It had been so long since I'd been able to dream or imagine feeling better. Thoughts of making such a drastic life change had always been met by fear about the further limits and struggle that I was sure would follow, and had been accompanied by an image of a dark void. I could not see beyond this void to anything truly positive, which is probably why I had held on so long and so tightly to my old way of being. However, the image of Jeannie and me rolling along on our peaceful walk, released from all the pressure and strain I had previously felt, was so great that I knew that it was worth letting go of everything to find.

I think a greater acceptance of myself, and the relief that came with it, was the key that made this transition eventually so life-giving. I was through resisting and no longer viewed letting go as giving up. I accepted how weak I had become and that I was now ready for a change. My perception of myself and my body's abilities had shifted. I had always believed I was just a seated version of

143

my non-disabled friends who simply needed to put in more effort than average to do the same thing. I now admitted to myself that I was not. My level of effort was not the only difference. I was truly satisfied that I had used every drop of muscle strength available to accomplish my goals, and felt I'd done it well. It was becoming acceptable to me now to view my physical body as disabled. This was a huge step for me.

My acceptance was further deepened at the end of that summer when, instead of returning to work, I attended an all-day conference on post-polio. I would never have considered this previously. In fact, I had always made a conscious effort to avoid hearing stereotypic profiles about polio because, even at a young age, I knew my thoughts influenced my body and I did not want to limit myself. However, I decided it was time to get more information.

The room was filled with people experiencing all levels of weakness, and I definitely was among the weakest. I listened intently, wondering how many of my experiences would coincide with the medical presenters' descriptions of my disability. Since I don't recall my muscles strengthening or remaining stable for decades like most people who'd had polio, I concluded early on that my body didn't follow the rules in this arena, either, and that few descriptions that day would probably apply to me. So much for my conclusions. First of all, I found it humorous that they listed a set of common personality traits for polio survivors as optimistic, strong-willed, type-A overachievers. Well, that certainly fit. Maybe that's why we survived, I mused. But as more information was given, my cocky attitude became more serious. Information regarding general nerve and muscle damage and overuse through the years certainly rang true, but when the list of almost a dozen post-polio symptoms appeared on the screen, I was shocked. These late onset symptoms fit me to a T. Apparently, five or more symptoms indicated the presence of this secondary condition, and to my amazement, I had nearly all of them.

I had read some of this information a year earlier, but something was different this time. Maybe it was the way it was presented, maybe it was the energy in the room, or maybe I was just ready for some deeper understanding and self-forgiveness. I suddenly realized that I didn't need to argue with my body anymore. It really *couldn't* do it. There was a sense of relief in labeling it all and in seeing that maybe I could not have stopped these physical manifestations after all. I felt remarkably validated by hearing about these very real symptoms, and the quiet but strong feeling that I could control my body by resisting and trying harder was washing away. I finally had a sense of acceptance and self-forgiveness, and was ready to go on from there. Fortunately, I would find avenues for improved health and well-being in the next few years even with these secondary disorders— probably as a result of my new ability to not resist them, but to accept them as real. Now that my old vantage point had shifted, I could relax a bit and invite a broader, stronger presence to arise within me to carry my physical form.

I am well aware that I did not draw such grand insights that day at the conference by myself. These were not my average thoughts. They were clearly of a higher order, freely given by Grace. For the first time I had an appreciation for what my body had done for me despite its increasing challenges. I no longer felt in opposition to it, but grateful for it. I also became very aware that, although I had a plate full of physical conditions, that I'd been, and still was, amazingly functional.

To experience this shift in perception was indeed a healing. I have had many healings in my lifetime brought by a variety of circumstances and experiences. Each time their purpose is the same: to unload narrowed, burdensome thought so that my true divine nature could well up more strongly to support me and ease life physically, emotionally, and mentally. Sometimes I asked for divine intervention to release old, limiting habits of thought, having experienced that this was far more effective than what I was able to do on my own. And often this was done for me, without my conscious request, by Grace. Both avenues remind me that a small amount of willingness on my part is consistently met with a strong, supportive response as the universe rushes in to heal. This "knowing" has enhanced my ability to feel peaceful in the toughest of circumstances, and to have a stronger trust that my needs can be met, and that I can enjoy life more fully.

I spent the next year learning to shift my focus inward even more. I practiced reading my body and its needs to find out what it could do rather than what I wanted it to do. I did not like what I found. For about two to three hours a day I could think through my fatigue before my thoughts were so unfocused that I became sleepy and needed to stop. I continued to feel systemically ill and completely drained, barely running on a trickle charge. My muscles were fatigued as well, but the brain fatigue was unquestionably the most debilitating. It seemed as though I had focused so much over the years that I had blown out that part of my brain, the brain that I had depended upon to run my life. I learned during the conference that the polio virus attacked and weakened some of the neurons in my brain and not simply the ones to my skeletal muscles. Damaged neurons and major, long-term over-focusing were the cause of this mental fatigue. I had often joked in the past that even if I could not move, I could be rolled into a classroom and still run the show. Not so now. There was no stamina left even for my brain. My "control tower" was down.

Days became simplified and self-reflective. For once I took my time to do the physical routines of the day without pressure from a rigid schedule. Even the thought of having any set schedules caused my body to feel strained. Fortunately, my parents were available to get me out of my chair several times a week in the afternoon to sleep, which helped ease the ingrained exhaustion. I've never been one to nap, but naps became essential. To bring in some lighter energy, I volunteered a couple of hours a week at each of my two schools that year for the enjoyment of being with the kids and my colleagues. It was just enough to feed my soul and give me a more gentle emotional transition into this new part of my life.

My willingness to connect to, and relax into Grace was strong. I knew that I no longer had the strength to push against the currents of life, and my only option was to let go and see where life carried me. There was relief in feeling that I was no longer in charge. I knew that good had come my way many times prior, that the universe knew I needed help, and that my needs were so great that I could not improve my life without a vast amount of divine intervention. I suppose I could have been angry or depressed and given up, fallen asleep spiritually instead of awakened, but the years I had spent seeking to work with life from the inside out apparently had given me enough of a foundation to trust that options could arise if I got myself out of the way. No dead-ends from looking with physical sight alone. I needed possibilities that arise with divine sight. I also knew that once the physical strain was gone, the emotional strain would lessen, too, and I would be in a better space to find good in whatever happened.

A need to work even more deeply from the inside out steadily pulsated through me in a quest to open myself to a realm of unlimited possibilities for good. I was drawn to daily meditation, something I had tried to incorporate for several years but had found little time for. Meditation continues to be a regular, vital practice that repeatedly quiets my mind and calls forth a palpably higher vibrational energy, my "high octane fuel," to help manifest health and get my needs met more smoothly. My ability to sense expanded divine energy and guidance, and feel more relaxed about life, grew as a result of consistent meditation, slowing down drastically, and having a brain that was too tired to think. This was an unexpected benefit that gradually breathed life back into me over the next few years.

Several other avenues appeared to support and enhance my connection to the divine. I discovered and resonated strongly with Doreen Virtue's *Archangel Oracle Cards* as a channel for connecting to the angelic realm for guidance as well as a sense of peace. In addition, one of my attendants mentioned a church service she had visited recently and suggested I attend because she felt it "sounded like me." I never imagined that in my mid-forties I'd be interested in attending church at all, but the Center for Spiritual Enlightenment sounded right up my alley. Now with fewer physical demands, I was able to afford a bit of strength to drive over and attend a service. I immediately felt at home. I liked the fact that they acknowledged and accepted all spiritual traditions, and that they emphasized the harmonious philosophies found at the mystical core of all major religions rather than their differences. The Center did not teach a specific religion, but taught practices of spiritual awakening appropriate to any religion based in the ancient Vedic disciplines and philosophies of Kriya Yoga (Yoga meaning "union with God"). My life's experiences dovetailed beautifully with the teachings, and I felt very fortunate to find such an unusual oasis so close to home.

I also began reading *A Course in Miracles: A Textbook for Students*, a channeled text of Christ teachings. The title had intrigued me ten years earlier and intuitively I knew that the teachings were important for me. However, I also somehow knew at the time that I was not yet ready to grasp and apply the vastness of its teachings. I had some other learning to do first. My logical mind actually found it odd that I would be attracted to Christ consciousness. Though I learned about Jesus during my Protestant upbringing, I had decided sometime in my youth to skip over Him completely in my prayers and talk directly to God. It seemed very logical to my young mind to go straight to the top! So to be drawn to these teachings was truly a surprise that was profound in shifting my perceptions towards greater Light.

I now felt ready and eager to read this work, covering only a few pages at a time for the next two years to let the book's teachings soak into my mind and shift my perceptions toward clearer divine thought. I drank in the words and experienced such periods of deep contemplation that I felt a transformation of beliefs occur. I noticed a base of more forgiving, kind thoughts emerge toward myself and my disability that also brought me greater forgiveness and compassion toward others. I didn't simply understand the concepts, I felt them deep in my soul, which allowed me to live more genuinely by them. The depth of the book's teachings for me was clearly greater than the sum of its parts. Of the many truths taught, four come to mind that significantly enhanced my belief system and brought me a greater sense of peace:

1. I was not *supposed to* know how to do life to my highest good. I was to ask for divine guidance, always, and trust that my actions with continued good intent would be led to their best outcome, always.

2. Instead of attempting to analyze/mold my current limited thoughts into something closer to Divine Truth, I could ask to have thoughts wholly (or perhaps "holy") replaced with thoughts already based in Truth, even when I was not sure what specific thoughts needed replacing. Essentially, I didn't need to wrestle the dragon to the ground over and over again. I could receive and assimilate new thought that didn't include the dragon at all.

3. All solutions have already been given.

4. There is no order of difficulty in miracles. All are equally accessible. I was familiar with these concepts through my readings over the years, but I had only understood them at an intellectual level. After two years of reading *The Course in Miracles*, I felt their trueness and their enlightening impact on my life.

In retrospect, this was a time of powerful spiritual growth that eventually opened me to a greater, higher flow of energy for creating life peacefully. Although I was at my weakest and most vulnerable state on the outside, I was growing exponentially on the inside. The dominant thought energy of my body, or habit of being, had to finish dying down so that a new way of thinking and being could arise. Many self-images had to be released. Well beyond my conscious awareness, profound changes were being made at the spiritual level to bring these manifestations to life. Only in retrospect can I appreciate the magnitude of this shift. I was not hit by a spiritual lightning bolt that suddenly changed me. In fact, nothing seemed particularly earth shattering at the time. I was just seeking some relief and trying to find who I was becoming. And miraculously, in the process, a space was created for my soul presence to shine forth more powerfully into the physical world and revitalize me. However, there was one more big change, also involving an image release that was to happen before I could begin feeling this new, stronger form of energy course through my body.

Chapter 18

More Loss, Greater Gain

Somewhere in this "die-down" period, my thoughts about my body, energy, and strength changed from unceasing depletion to gratitude and appreciation.

I had always been proud of the fact that I could drive. People were often astounded when they saw my physical weakness and learned I drove a full-sized van. It gave me an incredible sense of independence and joy to get around on my own. I loved the image of being someone who had achieved such mobility despite the severity of my disability. However, there were added pressures that came with driving with a body like mine and with the equipment I depended upon. There was self-imposed pressure to push my body to drive even when I was ill or feeling physically fatigued and there was pressure to quickly solve mechanical problems with the vehicle or its equipment to keep me "up and running." As my body lost strength, it seemed my focus and expense of energy became greater.

My new van, nevertheless, was spectacular. It had been a long road to get the adaptations funded through the Department of Rehabilitation, but years of persistence had paid off and the van I purchased to modify supported me better physically. The fine-tuning of the adaptations specifically relating to driving had been masterfully designed to better match my physical strength once again, and I thought I was set for quite some time. This was a van beyond my dreams.

However, my strength was changing so rapidly that within only two years I was struggling again. Driving had become such a part of who I was that the thought of letting it go was as difficult as my decision to stop working. The van was so easy to drive that it was hard for me to believe I could now only drive with great effort and only on a good day for a short period of time. It was no longer functional, and I knew it.

I thought a lot that spring about the need to stop driving. I did not want to be unsafe, but I had so many thoughts that were getting in the way. I could feel a strong tug inside that it was time to stop, but that I was holding on and not wanting to let go. I would have to let go of the image of being special because I could drive, let go of coming and going when I wanted, and face yet again how weak I had become. It felt like another great loss, and seemed to confirm that an increasingly limited life was inevitable.

But, the universe was waiting for me to make my move so that life could open up again, rather than amass more limits, as I had feared. I must have needed something wonderful to help me make the change, because the next events were so clearly heaven-sent to ease my transportation woes that I could not miss their significance.

I wanted to replace my old minivan, the one I could be driven in, with a newer, more reliable vehicle since I knew my driving days were numbered. I had several "chauffeurs" between friends and family for occasional rides. I wanted the freedom of having some additional mobility to supplement the rides I would be receiving locally through the county's paratransit program. I was in no position financially to make this purchase, but thought I could possibly cash in my small annuity early, pay the large penalties, and figure out the balance from there. I was at the beginning stages of planning, simply contemplating some options.

During the same time as my official retirement from the school district a couple of months later, I received a letter from my annuity saying I was *required* to begin withdrawing money because I was retiring. That meant no penalty! It was such a spectacular, unexpected solution, that I knew Grace was in motion. I was in awe of its appearance, comforted by its presence, and took it as a sign to relax and trust that this much needed gift was already unfolding. I literally guessed how much to withdraw monthly, relying completely on intuition, and a month later the first check arrived in my account.

Since the van conversion I wanted could not be found at a local dealership, I assumed it would take several months to find. However, to my great surprise, when I called the gentleman who serviced my van's adapted equipment to ask how to begin the process, he said that he already happened to have a new van he'd received a few months earlier that he was using as a demo vehicle until it was sold. The van was perfect and had everything I wanted, down to its beautiful, light blue paint! It was as if it were waiting for me, a heavenly special delivery, and it was by far better than I thought it could ever be. The financing was no less miraculous. When the final calculations were made at the bank, I beamed. The monthly car payment was almost exactly the amount of the annuity deposit—I had $2.12 to spare! Two weeks later, Jeannie and I were being driven in our new van to spend a few days at my parents' cabin at Tahoe. I was feeling exceptionally grateful for such a wonderful vehicle and for such an unexpected touch of Grace. It reinforced to me that I was on the right track, gave me another concrete example of infinite possibility and divine support, and strengthened my trust in life. This was a good time to receive such a blessing.

Now that I had a reliable vehicle for rides, my "knowing" that it was time to stop driving grew stronger. But as it grew stronger, my resistance grew stronger as well. Do I trust that life could get better and move on, or postpone the change a little longer for fear that life would be worse? I found myself enmeshed in an inner battle between trusting the abundance of grace and letting go, or going with what was familiar even if it did not feel good anymore. I felt emotionally and physically strained as my ego argued with the wiser part of my soul, resisting and fearing yet another change. This went on for a couple of months. I felt so tired of being at war with myself that one day it suddenly occurred to me that I had another choice: I could ask God to give me the willingness to let go of the need to drive and to bring me peace about my decision. I remember asking sincerely for help because I was being tormented by my own thoughts and did not want to feel that way anymore. I had learned during my time with Patricia years earlier that trying to force through my will only made my resistance stronger, so I needed to come at it a different way.

I promptly forgot about my request, but the universe did not. A couple of weeks later I drove my van for the last time. I had not expected it to be my last trip when I decided to drive to the mall to get my father's birthday present that day. I even stopped on my way home to get gas. The shopping had been quick, as usual, because I knew my strength would not last. As I pulled into my driveway and waited for my garage door to go up, I remember my thoughts suddenly shifting to a profound sense that I was done. The thoughts were clear, unshakable, and most importantly, met no resistance. The sadness and fear that I had felt around this change was replaced with a profound sense of relief. I closed up the van, put down the garage door, and went into the house to sit for a time with this feeling of peace and closure. It was while I was sitting there that I remembered my request for the willingness to let go. I was amazed how quickly my request to make this event peaceful, instead of traumatic, had been answered. I was deeply grateful, in awe once again at the magnificence of Grace, and relieved to have had such a connection. I knew I had received an immense gift to have been moved into this calm state, and I vowed that I would honor it by not entering the van again so I would remain clear with myself that I was done. I did not want to put myself back into emotional conflict.

I sold the van for the price of the vehicle alone to the same wonderful company who had modified it, requesting that they sell it to someone who could not qualify for funding. It was so specially modified that it needed to go to the right person, and I wanted someone to benefit from it who would not normally be able to afford it. The van was in mint condition, and this would allow someone with a significant disability to buy a phenomenal vehicle at a third of the price.

The van found a new home, and I decided to use the money to upgrade my well-worn kitchen as a gift to myself for letting go. This was the first time I had rewarded myself for doing something big, and the universe seemed pleased to oblige. I asked for divine guidance (my "angelic interior designers") to help me create my new kitchen on a limited budget and to my liking. I also asked for the right people to make it happen. To no surprise, everything fell into place. I even found a perfect kitchen table with the right height and configuration for maneuvering my wheelchair and feeding myself more easily. I now have gliding cabinet drawers I can actually open, the kitchen is bright and cheery, and people comment how inviting and peaceful it feels. The physical manifestations of the minivan and the kitchen, brought forth easily and providing such joyous relief, clearly indicated to me that I was on the right track of inviting life to flow again. I believe the key to opening the gate to this tremendous flow was letting go of my image of myself as a driver, which no longer served me. This took trust in divine possibility, and the will to hold to it, not to mention enough misery to want to make a change. They are daily physical reminders of the infinite goodness and power born of Grace.

I now became dependent on county paratransit, called Outreach, a local company that provides rides for those who cannot drive themselves, to go out independently in the community. I had resisted using the service because it was significantly more time consuming and more limiting than driving myself. However, now that driving was no longer an option and time was not so tight, the service was looking pretty good. It fit my need to get out independently, was reasonably priced, and I no longer had to worry about functioning alone when the weather was too hot or too cold, when my equipment needed repair, or when my muscles were too fatigued. I could relax and use the strength I had for the event itself, not for getting there and back. I did not have the stamina to go many places anyway, so this was perfect. It felt so good to get out consistently without effort. The rides also gave me an opportunity to see other disabled passengers who clearly had more difficulties than I. At least I could talk and think, I had some physical movement, and I returned to my own home at the end of the ride. It quickly put my losses into perspective, and set me thankfully back into the gratitude mode.

I wanted this last change to make a difference in alleviating my mental and physical fatigue. But after being off work a year and a half and not driving for two months, I remained constantly drained, my strength waning, and I was still limited to about three hours a day of minimal activity. I felt emotionally drained as well, though I knew this was not my normal state of being. Part of me was resigned to finishing life in this state, deeply satisfied that I had fully met my divine call to work with children. There was a peaceful sense of closure with that portion of my life, like I had successfully accomplished a divine agreement I'd made long ago. Yet another part of me was craving better health even if it was temporary. I had strongly felt that with my history of steady decline, the rate of my recent loss, and all of my current physical problems that I would not live more than a few years longer anyway. I can honestly say that I thought my job here on earth was done. I hoped the remaining years would not be physically brutal since I was on "suffer burn out," but that was still a real concern.

I decided to journal write for guidance, desperate for some relief from the fatigue. What I wrote that January day seemed possible I suppose, but only in hindsight could I see just how profoundly accurate it was. The writing was short and to the point, a question and answer format to the universe requesting some insight into my situation. I asked why I was still feeling so emotionally and physically drained, and waited to write the thoughts that soon followed. In response, I was told that my emotional and physical bodies were inextricably connected and that both energy bodies had to die down for something completely new to be created. I then had an image of the mythical Phoenix rising from its ashes, something I was only vaguely familiar with. I knew it had something to do with symbolizing spiritual rebirth.

I put the writing aside, feeling some sense of comfort from this insight but still feeling generally unsure. I wanted the information to be right and give some deeper purpose to my situation. I knew from previous experience that this information had come to me like other guidance and not regular thought: the idea was new and did not follow a chattering train of thought; it integrated seemingly unrelated pieces into a plausible whole, gave meaning and purpose to the situation in moving me toward good, and felt calming. Still, I needed to see proof to know for sure, so I decided to be patient and try not to make up my own not-so-Grace-filled story while I waited to see what played out.

A couple of months later, I began feeling better. I had longer periods each day when my body felt relaxed and I experienced clear thinking again. My eyes stopped their daily burning and tearing that had plagued me for many years and that I had only recently come to recognize as a sign of extreme fatigue. Most importantly, I felt a new, powerful flow of energy running vertically through the center of my body to replace the sense of collapse I'd been feeling for several years. I had never perceived that vertical column of energy until it collapsed and its absence was so notable, and I wondered if that was what people called "chi" or one's life force. This energetic tone, drawing me up from the earth into my physical form, felt as distinguishable to me now as my physical form. It literally felt as though I was being pulled upward by my chest bone with this energy, and it made me feel strong even though my muscle strength was weak. Lighting up my body, it provided a new kind of steady electrical "current" to my neurological pathways. My muscles, though weak, felt more alive and better able to perform consistently at their full capacity.

With this new surge of energy came a simultaneous uplift of emotions. I say simultaneous because I did not need the experience of feeling better physically before I felt better emotionally. Both systems lifted together as my guidance had said. I began experiencing not just the feelings of happiness or optimism that I'd known in the past, but also a deep sense of joy and peace emanating from my heart that needed no external event to trigger its arrival. In fact, nothing had changed outwardly, but clearly there had been a grand inner change that has continued to broaden and from which natural insight flows. It was as if my general vibrational set-point had been taken up a notch, and a greater portion of my soul presence was coming through to do life.

I felt as though a huge weight had been lifted, and that somehow I'd been turned back on. This time, however, I was far more careful with this gift of energy. The contrast between how I had been feeling and how I felt now made me extremely grateful for its return and far more respectful of it. Somewhere in this "die-down" period, my thoughts about my body, energy, and strength changed from unceasing depletion to gratitude and appreciation. Feeling good now had value. I felt good as long as I did not push myself, which I had learned to now recognize better, and I was more interested in treating my body well. This was a tremendous shift in consciousness. I had become more forgiving of my body and had learned some balance.

Back in the fall of that year, I had been visiting with my school district's superintendent when I felt a strong urge to ask him if I could work just a few hours a week on contract to do my favorite part of the job, bilingual speech and language assessments and consultation. I had no idea if this was possible physically or administratively, but I wanted to give it a try even though I still did not feel well. I knew working could be life-giving if I factored my body's needs this time into the equation. I thought I could manage about three to five hours a week and knew that the hours had to be extremely flexible based on how my body felt from day to day. This time my body was to lead. I could not force at all. My wish was granted, and I was given a contract to do the part of the job I'd loved but thought I would never be able to do again. I was back in my element with my colleagues and with students but at a level that was right for me physically. It was a fraction of what I had previously been able to do, but it was extremely satisfying and I felt useful once again. And with my upsurge of energy the following spring, I knew I'd made the right decision. I look back now and see that this was the beginning of new life spilling outwardly into my world.

Chapter 19

I Can't Breathe

I am often amazed at my body's tenacity for life. There have been so many times it could have said goodbye, which would have been a superficially easier solution for me, but obviously not part of my soul's game plan.

I was now ready to tackle the big issue of breathing, or should I say lack of breathing, while I slept. Beginning in my mid-twenties, I noticed that I needed to turn my head slightly to the right to keep my throat open so air could pass without being inhibited. It felt as though my weakened throat muscles somehow sagged when I fell asleep and narrowed the passageway, though my breathing was fine in the same position when awake. Since having my back surgery, I had been confined to sleeping flat on my back because I had no strength to turn over and this position kept my bones and muscles from aching. Changing body position to keep my airway open was not an option to help me breathe, so adjusting my head had to do.

In the early years I would wake up feeling as though I needed air, turn my head further, and that would suffice. But as the muscle tone and strength in my entire body decreased over the years, this became increasingly less effective and I was told I often had long pauses, sometimes close to a minute, between breaths. Only in later years did it wake me up and cause me conscious distress. The energy work I'd done with Patricia extended my body's ability to function at night this way, but it was clearly time to make a change. It had been an increasingly significant problem over the years, but in the last four years or so, every night had become a struggle. Elevating my head with the purchase of an adjustable bed frame had given relief for about a year, and then I was back to the same trouble from increased weakening. It took a couple of hours each night of falling asleep and waking repeatedly from lack of oxygen before I could finally remain asleep. To get my collapsed throat muscles to hold open a slight airway, I would employ a mixture of strategies, physical and metaphysical. I would affirm and visualize an opening, try to position my head as best I could, and/or ask the angelic realm to keep it open for me while I slept. If after two hours I was still not sleeping, I'd ask the angels to take me off to sleep so I could get some desperately needed rest. Inevitably with this request, I would miraculously fall asleep.

One of the benefits of attending the polio conference a couple of years earlier was seeing the term "obstructive sleep apnea" listed under post-polio symptoms. So that's what that is, I thought. I now had a label to what I'd been experiencing over the last two decades and realized it wasn't unusual for my type and level of disability. They also put a name to the extremely shallow nighttime breathing I was noticing when I did breathe, a central breathing disorder. Apparently, the "automatic pilot" part of my brain that tells my body to keep breathing when I sleep had been weakened by the polio virus, too, and essentially was worn out. This lack of breathing was in stark contrast to my strong ability to breathe while awake. It seemed obvious to me that my damaged neurological system had come to rely on my conscious presence to energize and direct it, and when I left in dreamtime, there was no one to fly the plane.

What they did not discuss at the conference was the panic that comes when a body is wired to survive. I became quite aware of my body's own consciousness and my cells' reaction to low oxygen and strain despite my desire to stay calm. I would awaken with a frantic feel of alarm and panic from my heart in particular, and that alone was exhausting to deal with. I wanted not to react so strongly since I did not see a choice, but my body definitely could not comply. There were several times when I finally was carried off to sleep, but the strain to breathe through an obstructed airway with weak chest muscles caused my heart and chest to feel deeply fatigued by morning.

Actually, I'm amazed I did not die during those nights. They were the worst, and I would spend the next day feeling rather detached with a sore, fatigued heart and chest muscles, and a sense that my heart was too tired to make it through the day.

Luckily, those severe nights were always followed by calmer ones. I constantly have conversations with the Divine during the day, and my interactions on those days were particularly strong, perhaps because the veil was thinned between life and death. I didn't say much to anyone in this world about these incidences. I had no need to discuss it with anyone but God. I would have been at peace with staying in my body or leaving, but I wanted no more suffering. I knew there were most likely bigger battles going on deep inside spiritually, and so I would ask that Grace take the lead. Since I could not judge the true significance of what was going on from my little human perspective, I needed to surrender to the One that always guided me to my highest good and brought forth miracles. I had not missed the miracles that had already occurred even in this darkness. I was well aware that I should have been toxic from the lack of oxygen at night, but I did not suffer the daytime sleepiness that is expected with this severe kind of sleep apnea. My heart should have been damaged from the strain, but it was not. The fact that I repeatedly was carried off to sleep despite my breathing difficulties over several years was miraculous as well and, of course, that I did not simply die.

I am often amazed at my body's tenacity for life. There have been so many times it could have said goodbye, which would have been a superficially easier solution for me, but obviously not part of my soul's game plan. My body definitely did not give up easily. As a result, each challenge has made me go strongly inward in search of a metaphysical, spiritual solution to relieve serious suffering. I wasn't going to get off the hook by dying. And if the truth were to be known, I have stated in my divine conversations over the years that I did not want to go back home without earning my "A+" because a "B" just wouldn't do. I've had comical images of arriving too soon at the pearly gates and hearing, "Wow, if you had just stayed a little longer, you could have gotten that A+. Instead you got a B+. You quit a little too soon. You were almost there!" I'm sure that scenario came more from my own perceptions than that of Grace, but nevertheless, it was true for me. I figured if I'd already gone this far in my spiritual development, I didn't want to stop short of the finish line. I wanted that grade. So in light of this, I decided to get some specific medical information to help clarify my options.

The specialist was knowledgeable and sincere. He was clearly concerned after hearing me describe my breathing at night, and seemed quite familiar with the scenario. Based on the type and severity of my disability, he felt that a tracheotomy and breathing machine for nighttime use was my only option. He would not support the option of a less invasive sleep apnea machine because I lacked nighttime care to pull off the mask if I got sick or if something went wrong. I thought his concern for my safety was valid since I had no movement to help myself with the equipment. Even if I had assistance, he explained, the apnea machine would not help the central breathing issues I described regarding my extremely shallow breathing anyway.

I listened to all the information carefully. I was aware when I scheduled the consultation that a tracheotomy would probably be brought up as a future option, but did not think I'd hear it was my only option and that it should be done without delay. Even though I thought I was prepared, the news hit me like a ton of bricks. I held the rush of terror at bay so I could rationally continue the conversation and get the information I had come for. If I had believed this was my only option, I doubt I could have separated myself in the moment from the emotion to remain in a problem-solving mode. I knew, thank God, with my past experiences that there was a possibility of improving my respiratory system metaphysically, and that knowledge kept me calm as we spoke in his office. I had wanted him to clarify my physical options so I could make an educated decision, and he had. There were no physical options that suited me. I now needed another miraculous outcome to arise, once again, born of Grace.

I declined a sleep study since I felt the results would only substantiate the need for a tracheotomy that I did not want. The doctor seemed worried about my decision, explaining that he had seen the suffering that came with slow anoxia. He racked his brain for another solution, but he knew of none. Although I truly respected his opinion, I knew it was not for me. I explained some of the improvements I had already experienced by directing my body through thought, including my swallowing, in an attempt to explain my choice and bring him some peace, too. I did not mention the other components to this process such as healings through the angelic realm, shamanism, or my own quest for divine truth and its relationship to health since I was sure these were too far reaching for him to consider real. He apparently did not have any experience using the mind/body connection for such difficult situations because my attempts to explain the most basic concepts brought him no relief. He was respectful, but I am sure he thought it was impossible. I thanked him for his knowledge, acknowledging that it was helpful even if it was something I did not want to hear. As he walked me out of his office, he kindly said that if I changed my mind he would be pleased to be my physician.

The consultation I received that day was invaluable. I was pleased that the universe had brought me a compassionate doctor who read my needs accurately and offered me honest help within the realm of his experience. After doing his best to alleviate my fears and present the value of his recommendation, he graciously accepted my decision to do otherwise and kept the door open in case I changed my mind. I was impressed by his genuine approach and obvious desire for my well-being, something that was unheard of in earlier years. He had no idea how emotionally healing our brief interaction had been regarding my relationship with doctors.

The information, though hard to hear, clarified my options. I could address the physical problem of breathing with a physical solution and resign myself to an unwanted outcome, or address it at a deeper, metaphysical level that could effect a healing and bring forth a miraculous outcome. The first option felt constricted, traumatic, and dead-ended, all too familiar feelings about dealing with my body in this lifetime. There was no hope for me in that solution and I truly felt there could be more. The second option felt expanded, joyous, and hopeful. This did feel right for me, and was the avenue I would pursue with all of my heart.

This was a huge undertaking, but my conviction was strong. There is nothing like matters that feel like life or death to tune my intention setting with laser-like focus. I wanted to breathe peacefully at night on my own so badly that I would settle for nothing else. If there is no order of difficulty in miracles, I reminded myself, then restoring the energy to support strong nighttime breathing was a viable option, and in reality, a solution already given by Grace. My job, therefore, was to adamantly align myself through my thoughts and emotions to this solution. I had experienced miraculous physical results by dealing with my swallowing problems metaphysically almost two decades earlier, so I knew it was possible. In order to make this possibility a probability, I knew this time I had to be wide open to allow a vast amount of healing to be brought to me rather than directing and driving the energy myself. I needed more divine help than I could orchestrate alone.

I spent time every day during my two-week visit to Lake Tahoe that summer in mediation grounding myself to the strength of the mountains, setting my intention to open my airway, and asking Grace to pour in. The thought of a breathing machine and the complications that would arise with having a hole in my throat made the discernment of what I did want rock solid. I was drawn to meditating with crystal stones to enhance my energy, something I had never considered before, which I think was also helpful. I sat with the energies of heaven and earth until I felt the idea that breathing peacefully at night without mechanical assistance was waiting for me. Once the belief and feeling were in place, I used my will and discipline over the next few months to hold them with unwavering faith. As thoughts of doubt or worry surfaced, I would breathe them out in the moment and ask to have them replaced with peace and possibility.

About the same time, I had an idea to ask the angelic realm to take me to "class" each night as I slept, a course in advanced spiritual awakening, to help bring forth this change in my body. I could not wait any longer to expand into the abundant energy of divine truth with stakes this high. My respiratory system was almost collapsed at night. I needed the energy of broader spiritual knowledge to flood my consciousness and be infused into my everyday thoughts to bring about health. A strengthening of my soul's presence in this body would provide the higher realm of possibility I was looking for, and learning while my ego slept seemed to me to be the most effective route.

So for nearly a year, every night before falling asleep I asked to be taken to class and to be seated front and center, promising to be a model student. I was encouraged by the familiar tingling "energy rush" that responded to my call each night as I fell asleep, and I knew I was in good hands. I was very comfortable asking and receiving this guidance, and had no doubt it would be of great help. It did not take long to see its benefit, and I feel it was one of the best decisions I have made regarding my own development. I would awaken during the night with insights streaming in regarding the perfect interrelatedness of all, glimpses of the spiritual purpose of events for myself and others, and a growing understanding that everything was righting me toward my greater good. In addition, I do believe it opened a pathway for the supportive intervention that followed and my ability to receive it well.

When I returned home that summer from Tahoe, Patricia referred me to a delightful, talented intuitive healer named Kristi who could work directly on this physical healing with me. The fact that Kristi lived in another state was not an issue, I was told, since she was accustomed to working "long distance" through the interconnectedness of the divine plane. Though this idea might be a stretch for some, I had no doubt it was true. I had experienced marvelous results with another intuitive healer several years earlier who significantly improved Zinkle's seizure disorder through long-distance healings. The issue of proximity, or space, was actually not an issue at all.

Kristi was another perfect match for me, becoming the fourth in a series of phenomenal women to support my spiritual and physical evolution. Her upbeat personality, ready laugh, and genuine desire to help, put me immediately at ease. Kristi had been a graduate of the Barbara Brennan School of Healing, but beyond that, it was clear to me from our first session that her skills and knowledge as a healer far exceeded that of only one lifetime. I realized by her insightful comments regarding my body, my energy, and how I functioned that her innate ability to connect to and work with the higher realms was magnificent. Her work with me once a month, in conjunction with Patricia's, would bring together the energies of heaven and earth to call forth improvements in my breathing and much more.

I had my last, serious nighttime battle with breathing in October, two months after beginning my work with Kristi. I was surprised that it appeared, since I had already enjoyed many nights of improved breathing that allowed me struggle-free sleep for the first time in years. But this was one of those unusually tough nights where dealing with exhaustion from lack of sleep paled in comparison with handling visceral fear and a struggle for life. It was as if something dark had to raise its head just one more time. My body's tenacity prevailed, but I spent the next day rather spacey with such a fatigued heart and chest muscles that it felt as though my heart might stop from exhaustion. Remarkably, I was not panicked about my situation. I felt tired but relaxed with a deep sense of peace, completely unattached to continuing life in my body or out of it. As I write this, I realize that this had been true for each of these events in the past, and a sign of the powerful infusion of Grace into my body. I was not dealing with this nightmare alone.

The soreness in my chest slowly subsided during the following day and I slept peacefully that night. The central breathing disorder, which was causing me to "forget" to breathe as I slept, also improved over the next couple of months with Kristi's amazing work, and my body relaxed. That was more than two years ago. Never again have I experienced another traumatic night without air. I have adequate brain signals for shallow but consistent breathing, and a sufficient, sustainable passageway in my throat to breathe peacefully throughout the night. I had remained open for a miracle and it had come.

There are no words to express the far-reaching relief that this brought. A seemingly impossible feat had been accomplished. More than just a physical improvement, it reflected a deep spiritual shift within me toward the unlimited possibility of consciously choosing life-giving energy to feed this body instead of unconsciously focusing on, and fighting against, a constant pull toward loss and death. I now had a feel for the difference in these energies. They are distinct. The first feels expansive, peaceful, provides options, and is life-giving regardless of the situation. The second feels dark, constricting, and dead-ended, to be endured until life is literally extinguished. This second, fear-based energy could not itself be changed into peaceful energy. The thought energy had to be *replaced*, and then the quality of the manifestations that arose from it became inherently different.

The desire to breathe sufficiently at night on my own had become a blessed reality, raising my awe and gratitude for my two earthly helpers and for divine intervention to new heights. I now believe that addressing my breathing was bringing to a close a lifetime dance between life and death played out through this scenario and many others in the past. The shift was so profound that within the next few months, I became aware that my mindset about living with my disability had been drastically altered. The ingrained beliefs about enduring a progression of increased weakness, suffering, and struggle as the only path to eventually leave my body were miraculously replaced with thoughts of living this last part of my life peacefully, and eventually when it is time for my soul to leave, that this process could be peaceful, too. These thoughts literally welled up effortlessly and felt unquestionably true without my conscious direction, clearly beliefs more in line with divine thought. I felt significantly less fearful and more relaxed about completing life with my disability, and the thoughts that have emerged from that mindset have been inherently more supportive of my own health and happiness.

Another unexpected gift of grace emerged about six months after my breathing stabilized at night. I began awakening from my dreamtime feeling the most beautiful, loving, blissful energy pouring into, and engaging with, my heart. I had an immediate awareness of the energy in my heart chakra, something I had never sensed before, and I felt a wide expansion of this energy as my love blended with its love. Words cannot adequately describe the experience, but it was an exponentially deeper love than anything I have ever felt on this earth. I'd had a flash of this divine love on two other occasions, feeling as if someone had followed me from my dreamtime to my waking time, but the engagements lasted less than a minute. Even that brief exposure was profound, and gave me a feeling of love, safety, and wholeness. There was no question about the purity of "its" intent. It held a great love for me, and I was awestruck by its presence.

This time, however, the presence was immensely stronger, recognizably loving and blissful, and had a male feeling to its presence. It was a good thing this occurred during spring break when I had few commitments. I remained in a deeply loving, blissful state for more than a week. It was hard to focus on just one world when I was simultaneously feeling two in such a loving way. The power of this love was so strong that it felt as though it had burst through something and had finally come to stay. And, indeed, it has.

It has been nearly three years. I now feel this loving exchange on a regular basis, and it is more sincere and real than anything I have experienced on this earth. Its consistently supportive, loving, energy connects my heart repeatedly to the wider expanse of the higher divine realms where all is well. I rarely speak of this "relationship," but it has so greatly deepened my own ability to love, trust, and feel compassion that I could not leave it out. This book is about the awakening, or the revealing, of my soul's presence while on earth, and this gift of divine love has been a grand opening for just that. I have since learned of the concept of "twin souls," the reunion of two complete/whole beings in divine partnership, for enlightenment. This energetic, telepathic connection may indeed be what I am experiencing, for it has revitalized me from the inside out with a pure, divine love that heals all. In this partnership, I feel as though I have been blessed with a personal emissary to the Divine. Our connection continues to deepen and grow, possibly at an even more rapid rate than if we were experiencing daily life and strife together with human egos battling for control. I have no desire to search for a physical embodiment of this love. It is already perfect and whole, and I am forever grateful for it.

Chapter 20

Kidney Stone Queen

My body has been the perfect laboratory over the years to provide me concrete "experiments" for learning that the energy of thought and emotion, imbued with Grace, heals.

A new pulse of strength was surging through my body at my core, holding me up and clearing my mind, even though my muscles continued to weaken. The more I worked on myself, the more fine-tuned my ability became to sense my inner energy, my physical body's energy, and the interrelationship between the two. I noticed a tremendous sense of life force continuing to arise within me along with the new vertical "power cord" that had arrived the year before. The energy felt so phenomenally stable and powerful that I was surprised my muscles did not follow suit. My energy, at least, was more predictable and I was able to engage in afternoon activities once again and still feel good as long as I paced myself.

There was still more to address physically that year, however. Each season was brought to a close with my body passing kidney stones. My body, so spontaneously reactive to my thoughts and beliefs, seemed to continue unloading the old as I was being moved toward a more peaceful state of inner being. Not a fun process by far, but a familiar one. Although I did regard myself as the Kidney Stone Queen, never before had I passed stones four times in just one year. Thank goodness I had a metaphysical avenue for help. Patricia's work repeatedly moved the stones through more quickly, Kristi cleared and strengthened the energy as well, and I practiced allowing whatever the beliefs were, obviously set in stone, to leave. My mantra for that year was "Let it go!"

Kristi mentioned that she intuitively saw large amounts of dark energy being released from this lifetime and from previous embodiments in succession during this process. It was a relief to get her spiritual view of these events. Her perspective strongly resonated with me as true and shifted my perception of the events as chronic, unwanted problems to a greater purpose for good. I could relax a little and even joke that instead of muttering a profane expletive each time the stones started, I should be shouting "Oh, yay!" This broader perspective reminded me that I often do not know from my little perspective on this physical plane what I am truly seeing, and reinforced for me once again the consistent efforts of Grace to right me into wholeness. The best I could do was get myself out of the way, take care of my body, and not make incorrect, negative assumptions that would impede the work.

It was during my third such event that I made another huge health decision. I had been experiencing severe menstrual problems, had become quite uncomfortable with large fibroids, and was anemic despite daily doses of iron. After dealing with the complications of this while also trying to pass stones one afternoon, I suddenly decided I'd had enough. Something had to stop, and I decided in that moment to pursue a hysterectomy.

This was entirely new thinking for me. I never believed I could have this type of "optional" surgery because the risk of intubation and anesthesia was simply too great. I feared losing independent breathing and/or swallowing if something went awry, and because my body was so fragile, surgery felt highly dangerous. Though the risks were very real, my changing perceptions of life, positive experiences with metaphysics and health, and a stronger flow of life force gave me a new kind of strength to meet the challenge and not allow fear to lead. It was my greatest spiritual opportunity thus far, to voluntarily face deep fears and beliefs about my body and consciously replace them with hope and a belief in wellness. My body has been the perfect laboratory over the years to provide me concrete "experiments" for learning that the energy of thought and emotion, imbued with Grace, heals. In fact, it is the only factor that has consistently moved me toward a good outcome, no exception, and has yielded the clearly miraculous results I needed. It is my ability to consciously connect to this divine healing energy that turns fear into courage, and improves my quality of life.

The decision came quickly and felt absolute. It would take all of the skills and knowledge I had acquired using thought, emotion, energy, and divine truth to assure a favorable outcome for such a serious endeavor, and I was ready. I knew that this time my will could not be used to force or drive an outcome. Instead, I would use its strength to hold an opening for receiving the healing energy of the universe by adamantly affirming and believing that there was indeed an option for good. Holding my thoughts steadily in this direction, I trusted, would summon a strong current of Grace to align all and carry me to a safe, healthy outcome.

I made an appointment with my gynecologist of many years, a man whom I respected as a person and as a physician. I am sure he was quite shocked when I announced that I was ready for a hysterectomy. I had always wanted to avoid surgical procedures at all costs, and now I was ready to jump in with both feet! I told him all the reasons why I believed it was time for a hysterectomy. I also explained that I had learned to work well with my body energetically from the inside out to help it along, that I felt completely confident that he was the right man for the job, and that I was sure the outcome would be good. He was not so quick to share my enthusiasm, however. He was well aware of my previous fears about surgery and the increased risk factors that came with my disability (10-12% instead of 1/2% for this type of surgery). He wanted me to proceed more slowly and consider a less invasive procedure instead of abdominal surgery.

I agreed to have a consultation for another type of procedure first. The results of the visit were even more clarifying for me. During the consultation I realized there were risks and complications with this procedure as well because of my disability, though less than abdominal surgery, and it did not guarantee that the problem would be completely solved. The "alarm bells" went off in my head when the physician talked about the procedure as if I were able-bodied, never once asking specific questions about my disability as it related to surgery or recovery. This felt like a prime prescription for another medical disaster with a physician who did not see me clearly.

I spoke with my gynecologist again, telling him my concerns about the other procedure and the physician. He listened carefully, and even though I'm sure he had hoped for an easier option for me, he agreed to surgery. His awareness of my needs, his genuine concern for my well-being, and willingness to support me simply confirmed that I was in good hands. I am grateful that he wisely proceeded with caution but did not succumb to fear so that I could have better health.

There was the physical aspect of preparing for surgery, including appointments with specialists and a variety of tests, but this held a small portion of my attention compared to the metaphysical, soul-connecting aspect of the process from which I knew all else would arise. I had chosen to tread into potentially dangerous waters, so to speak, for the option of attaining better health and quality of life. The stakes were high, but the light of my soul had been progressively strengthened by each previous experience to support me as challenges became greater. I truly believed, from personal experience, that I was not alone navigating these deep waters.

I needed to lower my still-present inner resistance from memories of past medical disasters so that a higher dimension of divine energy could radiate through me. This was where I knew my own work lay. I spent the next two months in spiritual preparation attuning myself to divine possibility and the energy of healing. Sitting in my backyard garden, I meditated in search of peace regarding the surgery. I did not leave meditation each day until I felt that a good outcome was divinely guaranteed. As each fearful thought arose, and there were many, I'd offer them up for a healing from my heart and ask to have them replaced with divine truth. Some fears were quite strong, especially related to my breathing, but I would wait until I literally felt the stinging energy of fear release and be replaced with an expansive upwelling of calmness. It was an extraordinary experience to interact with the angelic realm so directly as fear was replaced with peace, and to feel, upon my request for help, such a clear, definitive shift in my emotional energy.

I had a great sense of emotional calmness and strength throughout the months before surgery. I remained focused on what I wanted instead of what I didn't want, especially when my surgeon attempted to bring my attention on more than one occasion to the added risks and possible complications because of my disability. He was doing his job as a good physician to educate me so I could make an informed decision about surgery, but I knew better than to focus my attention there, even for a second. I had already made up my mind about surgery and now needed to hone in my attention on only the positive.

He appeared to interpret my lack of reaction and attention to potential problems, however, as naiveté or possibly blind ignorance and finally blurted out one day that he was having a little trouble with my "Pollyanna attitude." It appeared I was stressing out this normally calm man. He obviously cared greatly for my well-being, and I realized it scared him to think that I wasn't getting the big picture, specifically the dangers. After I explained that what he was observing was essentially purposeful discernment on my part, not ignorance, to direct my body toward a healthy outcome, he seemed to relax just a bit. He had, indeed, done his job in advising me. He did not need to tell me about what to fear. I knew it well, having lived in this body and having experienced disaster. I understood. However, I also knew how my thoughts and emotions immediately affected my body's health, so I could not go there, into those thoughts, with him. Since we did not share the same experiences, I don't think he necessarily believed that my purposeful focus had such an impact on my body, but he understood that it was important to me and respected it.

I tried to approach everything related to the surgery from my heart rather than my head, from my presence rather than my egoic mind, to allow and feel the loving energy of the Grace that I'd come to recognize lead so I could follow. In addition to meditation, during all medical visits I sought inner guidance and support in the moment, asking to bring the right people into place, to give them insight, and for my body to do well. It was such a relief not to be in charge, but to yield and be led by wisdom. And as I steadfastly sat with divine possibility, I saw signs regularly even while in the hospital that I was being heard.

The anesthesiologist, a key player in this surgery, was experienced, reflective, and obviously brilliant. He was aware of my needs, was not afraid to work with me, and I felt he was intuitive in his work. The pulmonary specialist was delightful and equally gifted. He was genuinely pleased with the strength and clarity of my breathing while awake despite my overall weakness. At the end of the initial exam, he made a profoundly intuitive statement about my situation and I knew he was the specialist for me. "You may need to be on a ventilator for a day or so after surgery until you become fully present again to direct your own breathing," he said. "Don't worry if it's needed for a bit." I was thrilled to hear him make such an insightful comment acknowledging the important influence of will on my body's functioning, and knew what he said was completely true for me. I was pleased to have his expertise available, and was comfortable entrusting my breathing to him and to the anesthesiologist. Even the general practitioner that my gynecologist selected to work with me for the surgery was uniquely perfect. To my surprise, he had firsthand knowledge about polio from living with his brother. For once I was not the one doing the educating! I felt solidly good with all of the physicians and their ability to make wise decisions for me in the moment if needed.

In addition to having physicians in place to support my body from the outside, I lined up support to work from the inside as well. I asked friends for their prayers to strengthen the flow of divine energy in and around me. Kristi was set to work long distance at an energetic level throughout the surgery to keep my airway open and my breathing stable. Patricia would come into the ICU that afternoon to clear and charge my energy field, to essentially reawaken my field and jump-start my physical healing after surgery. It was such a gift to have this option of support, a wonderful avenue that always yielded such good results for me. My team was now complete.

My doctor did everything in his power to prepare for my hospital stay, blazing a trail ahead of me so that my many needs would be met. He talked directly to the hospital staff personnel on my behalf, arranged for a specialized call button for patients who have little movement, and secured a private room with space for my wheelchair and the option, if I would like, for a family member to stay with me while hospitalized. Jeannie, my dog, would also be welcomed to stay.

His diligence and kindness in looking after my needs made me feel safe and protected, an experience so very different from the traumatic ones of old. This medical experience was clearly emanating from a higher realm of divine energy where wholeness and peace lay. I was well aware that this surgery was not just about a physical healing. I was practicing my ability at a deep level to work with life metaphysically, to bring the healing energy of Grace directly into my physical experience where darkness stood and call forth light. And in the process, I would receive a deep clearing of old fears and emotions, to be replaced with something more in alignment with my greater soul-presence and my highest good. My ability to trust doctors and trust life was receiving a healing once again.

By the time I arrived at the community hospital to check in the night before the surgery, I felt incredibly strong and peaceful within. There was nothing left to do but let go and calmly allow the process unfold before me. I felt profoundly aligned with divine will, and with that came great trust and an openness to any outcome. This experience was clearly imbued by Grace, and because I felt its presence and strength, I trusted it would lead me into goodness.

Much to everyone's relief, I was off the ventilator right after surgery and breathing on my own; the surgery had gone extremely well. The work of several months was complete and I was thrilled with the outcome. The hardest part was over. As long as I was breathing independently, I knew the rest would heal. I continued to work with the divine realm to ensure a smoother recovery in the hospital even as I awoke. I noticed some congestion in my lungs, which is normal after anesthesia but a large problem with my extremely weak cough. It made me nervous to know I had no strength to clear it by myself, so I immediately asked for the divine realm to help clear it with me, and within a few minutes, it was miraculously cleared with one small cough. Thank goodness I was so practiced in working metaphysically this way. Being proactive as soon as I became conscious certainly helped things along.

My doctor, with kind but concerned eyes the night before surgery, was now grinning from ear to ear. He was extremely pleased with how well I had done. The pulmonary specialist came into the room next exclaiming, "Look, how beautiful! You did it!" and kissed my forehead with delight. What a lovely response from both of them. With the exception of intestinal pain for several days as that part of my body regained itself, everything went smoothly over the next few days. I needed much less pain medication than expected, another sign for me that healing energy was strongly flowing through my body. The staff at each part of my stay was kind, responsive, and highly professional. Their willingness to listen and work with me in partnership was unprecedented. The entire event played out perfectly, and six days later, I left the hospital content and relieved. This indeed had been a healing experience on multiple levels.

I thought I was home-free, but three weeks later there was a seemingly unrelated problem that rose up without warning. I say "seemingly" because they were unrelated physically but most likely related metaphysically as old energy was clearing to make way for new. The fourth set of kidney stones that year tried to pass. However, this time a massive stone lodged and backed up an infection into my kidney and bloodstream. By the time I entered the hospital, I could no longer move and was seriously ill. This was far more life threatening than my surgery. I didn't give one more thought to my hysterectomy, as all of my focus was now needed to navigate this new situation. There was no preparing ahead metaphysically this time. I would have to blend the physical and metaphysical worlds moment by moment as I worked with the doctors to clear the infection and move through the medical procedures safely.

It was a rough road, but eventually the infection passed and the stone was removed. Because of the severity of the infection and a complication with the anesthesia during one of the procedures, I was not free from the stone for over a month. I had to work diligently at staying as open and calm as possible, knowing this was the best way to support my body and bring forth the best outcome. No more disasters. My body, just having come off of a major surgery and from combating the infection, felt drained and eventually so was my stamina for handling problems. I needed life to calm down. A six week anticipated recovery from the initial surgery had turned into three months of intense medical dealings and recuperating. I eased back into my part-time work schedule after the three months, but it was three more months before I could truly say I felt well.

Even though the stones may have served to clear out old energy, the intensity and seriousness of the infection were sure signs that something was way out of balance in my life yet again. My strong, "doing" personality had slowly found a foothold after retirement, and I found myself being far too busy using the little strength and stamina that I had. Since I was doing only a small fraction of what I used to do, I felt justified in thinking my body should be able to keep up. The kidney stone blockage was a painful motivator for me to look at this with spiritual sight, and I realized I was still engaging in my old habit of forcing action through my body with my will. Same propensity to force, it seemed, but with a smaller ability to make action. I sat with it, asking for guidance and being surprised at how aware I became in noticing the subtle difference between what felt open and what I was resisting. Although I still enjoyed it, my flow of "high-octane" energy had decreased for working with children, but felt more open for a different kind of teaching. The energy had shifted toward metaphysical teaching. My body, a reactive sensor to my alignment with divine energy, was a clear indicator that I must shift my focus toward this higher level of "fuel" to support my body.

I could not afford to force or resist, as this unconscious pattern was pinching off the very life force I was seeking. I had actually dabbled in writing this book after getting some direction during an amazing intuitive reading I had won from Colette Baron-Reid six months before my surgery. However, I had not made it a priority so it was barely off the ground. I had repeatedly drawn a "Change of Career" card from my divination deck as well, but it had seemed too unbelievable. A new career? I was too weak and exhausted. How could I possibly do something else when my body had so little left even for basic, daily functioning? I resisted the concept initially, telling the universe that there was simply no way. However, the same card appeared so many times that it became comical, and I knew a way would be found that was divinely perfect and supportive if I would just relax. I had no idea what the career change would be or how I would do it physically, but I was willing to be open to its possibility. About week and half after the surgery itself, I awoke early in the morning receiving an intuitive "download" for more than two hours about the spiritual purpose of my surgery and the medical experiences thus far. I was to teach others, using the experiences of my life as concrete examples, how to blend the two worlds for better health and a more peaceful existence.

I made some changes, including the decision to let go of my license as a speech pathologist. A major image release for me, since my whole persona still centered around being a speech/language therapist, but I knew it had to be done. I would still keep my school credential active but no more private work outside my school district. In reality, I was too weak anyway, but would have held on to the image if I had not experienced health problems each time I signed up for the continuing education units to maintain my license. I had paid for, but been unable to attend, several workshops that year and was trying to squeeze in an online class before the deadline when this last kidney stone episode arrived. I felt I had worked hard for that license, but it was time for a change in how I defined myself. I shredded the renewal paperwork, and after a month I began writing.

Chapter 21

Grace, Grace, the Divine Presence of Grace

*The body that I had tuned out for so many years turned out
to be the instrument with which I physically feel
the guidance and love of the Divine.*

It is true that I am the weakest I have ever been, but I am also
the most peaceful I have ever been. And with that peacefulness, options open and I am able to do life well. This past year has been the
calmest I have ever experienced both physically and emotionally,
and a much-needed respite. People often comment on how well I
look, even shortly after being so seriously ill with a blood infection.
I can only conclude that they are perceiving the light of my soul
emanating outward, now a little stronger, rather than my physical
form grown weaker.

I may always have to spiritually practice the art of balancing
action with beingness, which has played out so concretely in this
lifetime as balancing my strong will with my body's needs. It is still
not natural for me to know my physical limits, but I am kept in check
by reminders, sometimes quite painful, through my body's health or
lack of it. It is a physical meter that I am learning to value rather than
resist, a meter that reflects my alignment to divine thought and the
foundation that assists all aspects of my life in a Grace-filled way. I
am less apt to fight against my body now, but genuinely respect it for
its honesty about what I am creating for myself in life.

My innately optimistic view of life has been well tested and my
will has been tempered with wisdom through this physical body of
mine. This was essential to turn my belief system from thoughts of

having to resist and endure an unpreventable contraction of body energy toward death to a new, ever-increasing knowledge of how to navigate and call forth the expansive, healing energy of Grace to open life and support my whole being. The less rigid and limiting my thoughts have become about how I do life with my disability, the gentler I have become with myself. As a result, my body is better able to function with very little movement and I find solutions to my needs in amazing ways. The body that I had tuned out for so many years turned out to be the instrument with which I physically feel the guidance and love of the Divine. The deeper I connect, the calmer I am and the better my quality of life becomes despite the types of situations that arise, and the more this goodness spills out effortlessly to help others as well.

My body's intense reactions to my thoughts and how I treat it have kept the fire to my tail to pursue seriously spiritual awakening while on this earth in order to make sense of life, to lessen suffering, and to create a peaceful, happy, purposeful existence. Thank goodness for the many joys I have experienced in work, with my dogs, and with my family and friends that has flourished with little effort. I needed that joyous, unforced energy as a base while working on my relationship with myself, or better stated, my relationship with my (divine) Self.

I was always taught to be appreciative of the little things in life, but my awareness of the daily blessings of life is stronger and my gratitude for them has grown immensely. The struggles I've had gave me contrast to deeply appreciate when life is flowing well and a growing desire for, and belief that, unlimited goodness is the basis of all life. It continues to teach me how to access the beautiful power of Grace to actively co-create life with the Divine in a very functional way. My relaxation into this partnership, to feel it in every cell of my body, far surpasses logical thought, is inexplicably freeing, and brings forth miracles.

I have learned that the challenges that arise in life are not to just be endured, blindly accepted, or resisted. Their purpose is to stir our consciousness to really take a look at, and take a stand for, how we want to live our lives from a place of peace. Instead of looking at a challenge as overwhelming or a depressing dead end, it can be viewed as a signpost to direct us to adjust our perceptions toward a space more in line with spiritual truth by unloading heavy "thought baggage" that has caused suffering. The light of the soul then emerges a bit stronger with no special effort on our part since it is the true essence of who we are.

Energetically, the size of my "problems" has correlated directly to the amount of correction needed to adjust my trajectory towards my highest good. The difficult situations I've consistently had served to clear out that "thought baggage," those repetitious thoughts and beliefs of mine so rigidly held and strongly justified that impede the natural flow of Grace. I learned eventually to see that even what I thought was "bad" had a purpose for good. Sometimes I needed something really unpleasant to make a turnaround and go in the opposite direction toward wholeness.

I have seen in my own life how adversity can either cause us to fall asleep spiritually into a contracted state of fear or awaken us into an expanded state of peace. It is ours for the choosing. I believe our job as humans is to wake up enough to see the sacredness in every situation, most especially the difficult ones, and to set our intention with our will to hold open an avenue for Grace to arise. With that expectation of divine possibility comes the wisdom to acknowledge that our little selves cannot do things alone, nor can we judge from our limited physical perspective what is truly best in the big scheme of things. However, we do have the ability to ask that situations be guided by Grace, the One who does know. By trusting that options for good are forever present and arrive in perfect order, we learn to ask for and focus strongly upon the goodness that surrounds us and celebrate it. Out of this steadfast desire for Grace, a genuine sense of gratitude wells up and life becomes powered by an immense, un-hurried energy that brings forth great things. This inner strength, clearly felt through the heart, pours out to meet the world in a calm, confident manner. Its pulse is felt easily in the joys of life, and is sought out by us in the more difficult times to bring gentleness and peace to any situation. This pulse, or life force, is always present but the challenge is to remain connected to it during dark times. Instead of retracting from darkness, we can learn to use our larger, divine essence to move into and to light up any situation, all the while asking for and connecting to Grace. It is in this engagement where fear melts into courage and we find our experiences to be life-giving.

Living with a physical disability has served to deepen my continuous awareness of, and interaction with, the Divine for creating all aspects of my life. It has been the perfect situation to stimulate a mental quest for understanding the positive, expansive nature of Life and has helped me repeatedly find solutions and relief when there seemed to be none in sight. Esoteric contemplation of the metaphysical and physical worlds without action would have been intellectually stimulating but not life-altering. True learning, true knowing, has come from repeated, direct application in real-life situations where my will to persist rather than succumb to fear has been invaluable. It is in these experiences as we seek spiritual understanding to make sense of life that metaphysical practice, mixed with faith, become proven personal realities and wisdom is born. We then become the vessel of light that our soul longs to be, a portal for Grace to emanate into the world, bringing light into darkness, and peace to all things.

I am grateful that I was inspired to look inside for answers to my physical challenges. Never did I consider that it would be a spiritual quest or a profound healing from the inside out, the kind that gently and joyously opens life to a level that is more peacefully solid than could ever be imagined. It is not that my body has miraculously changed or that my needs related to it have disappeared. On the contrary, I have more physical needs than ever before. However, I am better able to approach them from a deepened inner perspective of divine possibility that solves all in a peaceful way. I now feel more solidly relaxed, life is more balanced, and I see evidence daily of how the interplay between the energy of my thoughts and the energy of world around me opens doors to the kind of out-of-the-box options and solutions that do not present themselves with logical thought alone. This has relaxed me about life and I no longer hold the subtle but diffuse fear of the future that I once had. When fearful thoughts do arise, I am better able to right myself into divine possibility and into a trust that I am being divinely led and supported at all times. I feel a calm expectation for good and a deep appreciation of the wise flow of life.

We all have joys and challenges that teach us who we really are as souls, not just bodies and personalities, if we know how to look. The joys are easy but do not usually spur us to look below their surface. It is the challenges that offer us the potential to deepen spiritually, though we often resist them because we think they should not be happening to us. Ironically, the harder we resist, the more it dampens the flow of Grace that we so desperately need to open life for us again.

I encourage you to look at yourself and your experiences in life through spiritual eyes, to see them as richly symbolic road markers on an inevitable pathway toward an awareness of your true soul's nature and the peace of God. What have your life experiences taught you about yourself? Did they deepen your compassion? Teach you discernment? Did you focus only on the details of your problem and miss the good that was there as well? Do not allow fear to attach so strongly to your thinking that a perception of "bad" is all that you see, because you are sure, then, to miss the Grace that also arrives with it. Be adamant about finding the good and leave the rest. You will soon see how you are already carried strongly by Grace and your appreciation of it will expand you further into its flow.

Because I have been so limited physically, I have had extensive "hands-on" practice in consciously blending the metaphysical and physical worlds so that I can exist more fully upon this higher, healing energy of Grace for literally everything I do or need. There are a few main concepts that have been key in developing my ability to navigate the world in this way:

1. *The universe is a powerful flow of healing, divine energy that supports all life.*

It is the true essence of life. Because we are all emanations of this greatness regardless of religious preference, we are inherently connected to it. As a spark of the Divine in physical form, we are a source-point in the world from which Grace flows that not only supports our well-being, but also spills out to those around us. The aperture of this divine flow is enhanced by our purposeful intent to call it forth through the energy of our positive thoughts and emotions. Take responsibility for honing and directing clear intentions for divine possibility, most especially during dark times, and do not waver. This ability to hold open an avenue for Grace to enter is the real purpose of our will. In conjunction with the proper use of discernment, a clear "yes" and a clear "no," it becomes a powerful source for calling forth Grace and a joyous expansion of life.

2. *Ask, ask, ask! We cannot see what is in our best interest or the best interest of those around us from our limited perspective.*

Trust that if you ask for help or guidance, whatever unfolds is moving you towards good even if it does not seem so at the time. Ask during prayer. Ask in the moment. Ask for the willingness to be willing. Question your own thoughts which may be in opposition to what you're asking for and could be slowing the process. Offer any negative emotions up for a healing from your heart, to be replaced with positive thoughts and emotions more in alignment with Grace. Build a pathway for divine engagement in everything you do as you move through the day, not just during a structured time of prayer. You will be amazed at the results.

3. *Develop your intuition so communication between your mind and your innate Divine Self opens into a two-way conversation.*

Notice how guidance and insight come to you. Notice slight shifts in your body's "feel." Divine guidance and insight are not luxuries for the select few nor are they paranormal, bizarre phenomena to fear. They are a natural, essential component of your current communication skills for the physical world extended into the metaphysical, Grace-filled world.

4. *Be open to a divinely-guided outcome.*

Letting go of details regarding how we think something should play out opens us up to greater possibility and results far superior to anything we could have imagined alone. Go back to experiences where life went well, those wonderful, effortless gifts of Grace that we say were "meant to be." Feel the strong, joyous, open energy of it. Focus on it and be grateful. Practice the feeling and sense of this Grace-filled energy of light and of your gratitude for it, so when times get rough, you know this feeling and can use it to better connect and maintain a strong expectancy of finding Grace again. The more you notice and appreciate life, the more your personal experiences will fortify your trust that outcomes are indeed being divinely guided.

5. *Believe that Grace-filled, miraculous options are not only possible, but they are already given and trying to come your way.*

They are as present in the universe and as obtainable as the many other, less favorable, choices that we think we are limited to having. The practice of asking for divine intervention, "... that, or something better" as I've heard Doreen Virtue say, is my favorite statement to open my thinking to great possibilities that are beyond my everyday thinking.

6. *Physical ailments are not separate, unrelated earthly by-products of a spiritual being trying to move through life in a physical body.*

They hold many messages for us about various parts of our inner self, as does our well-being, if we learn to look. Since our body's health is inextricably interwoven into our thoughts and emotions, it is a concrete indicator of that energy. Find support in any way that feels right to you to enhance the body's natural desire to move towards health. There are many avenues now available in energy and body work. Find what works for you. The clearing of dense energy not only helps physically but also over time brings forth thinking and emotions more in alignment with divine thought when we approach this consciously.

7. *Potentially, our greatest challenges bring forth our greatest spiritual learning and the release of old thought patterns that no longer serve us.*

It is helpful to see these challenges as having meaning and purpose for good. Consider the challenges as energetic clearings and try as much as possible to approach them with the purpose of "letting go" rather than pure resistance. Some issues may clear before they manifest into physical form through meditation and intention-setting and some won't. Either way, it is a clearing, and if you are present enough not to make a negative story about what is happening, you are less likely to add more dense energy to unload later.

8. *The less you resist or force life situations, the more open you are for Grace to flow through you.*

The development of clear discernment through asking and receiving spiritual guidance (a clear "yes" and a clear "no") is not resistance. It creates a permeable boundary that allows the higher, healing energy of Grace to enter and screens out the denser, lower energy of negativity. Be aware of what doesn't feel right or good to you, but don't stop there. Beware of being side-tracked by complaining. This is fragmented, dead-end energy. Let this help you instead to define what feels right and to give you clarity, and then place your focus there.

9. *Know your strengths and use them in service of yourself and others.*

This is what you have come to share in the world and is unique to you. This is a natural river of Grace.

~~~~~~~~~~~~~~~~~~~~~~~~~~~~~~~

I have not usually been one to talk about the trials of my life or share in detail my emotional and spiritual development with others, but I have been drawn to do so with this book as an aspect of my life's purpose. It is my deepest hope that through my story you will be inspired to see your own life story from a broader perspective for good, and choose to consciously bring that goodness of Grace into your everyday life.

I turned fifty last year and it feels formidable. It is an achievement to be functioning as well as I do at this age, to still be of service to others, and to feel emotionally solid after a lifetime of dealing with a severe disability. Most importantly, I feel closely engaged with my Divine Self, and that brings inexplicable peace. My body is weak but it is carried by my own Divine Presence of Grace, now so much stronger.

Breinigsville, PA USA
30 June 2010
240884BV00006B/62/P

9 781935 125297